PRAISE FOR *GOD OF THE UNDERDOGS*

You will love this book. Matt's unique way of storytelling will engage you from page one and leave you inspired to live up to your full potential!

—MARK BATTERSON, *NEW YORK TIMES* BEST-SELLING AUTHOR, *THE CIRCLE MAKER*

Matt is a new voice in leadership and one you need to listen to. The underdog message has been a common theme in my life for sure. My background was never in conferences and events, but here I am, leading the Catalyst Movement, primarily as an underdog. If God can use me, he can definitely use you. Matt's book will inspire you to take on the next challenge and be the leader God has called you to be.

—BRAD LOMENICK, PRESIDENT AND LEAD VISIONARY, CATALYST CONFERENCES; AUTHOR, *THE CATALYST LEADER;* @BRADLOMENICK

Everyone loves an underdog. In this book, Matt Keller shows us that God does too. In fact, God desires to use your shortcomings—and your failures—as a springboard to greatness. *God of the Underdogs* will guide you beyond your limitations and into a realm where only God-powered potential exists.

—JOHN BEVERE, AUTHOR AND SPEAKER, MESSENGER INTERNATIONAL, COLORADO / AUSTRALIA / UNITED KINGDOM

If you have ever had doubts, been fired, or want to do great things you've got to hear what Matt has to say.

—CAM CAMERON, FORMER HEAD COACH, MIAMI DOLPHINS; CURRENT OFFENSIVE COORDINATOR, LSU TIGERS

Matt's fresh approach to leadership and life will infuse you with courage. *God of the Underdogs* reminds us that no matter what comes against us, God is for us. I repeatedly found myself in the pages of this book, and Matt brought me through it with renewed boldness for Christ. This book will help you and your church step into the new opportunities God has waiting for you.

—TODD MULLINS, LEAD PASTOR, GOCHRISTFELLOWSHIP. COM; CHRISTFELLOWSHIP.TV

As a fellow underdog, I can relate to the need to follow the Lord even when you are totally convinced you are unqualified and unprepared for where He is leading you. *God of the Underdogs* is a rally cry for all of us to stop doubting our leadership and start trusting the Lord.
Everyone can relate to the feeling that they are unqualified to lead successfully. *God of the Underdogs* uses well-known stories of famous underdogs in biblical history and allows us to not only see them in a new light, but to see ourselves in them.

—ROB HOSKINS, PRESIDENT, ONEHOPE, INC.

God of the Underdogs is a message that our world desperately needs. There are many obstacles and challenges that stand between us and where God desires for us to be. *God of the Underdogs* will motivate you to overcome life's greatest challenges and reach your God-given potential.

—HERBERT COOPER, SENIOR PASTOR, PEOPLE'S CHURCH.TV, OKLAHOMA CITY

The mere sample of Pastor Matt's book left me wanting so much more. His book so beautifully illustrates this simple fact: God is for you. This book will challenge your excuses and inspire you to reach all that God has for your life. Do yourself and those around you a favor and pick up this book. You will be refreshed by story after story that prove you have what it takes to do great things for God. Get it, read it, and change the world.

—PASTOR ROB KETTERLING, LEAD PASTOR, RIVER VALLEY CHURCH

Great book! I believe the Lord will use Pastor Matt Keller and *God of the Underdogs* to give you hope to overcome any obstacle that stands between you and the greater purpose that God has called you to. Keep your eye on this young pastor. He will change the world.

—PASTOR RICK BEZET, SENIOR PASTOR, NEW LIFE CHURCH

One of Satan's favorite tools is to convince us that we are unworthy, unuseful, unqualified to lead. As an underdog, surely targeted from my earliest days for destruction, I've been surprisingly redeemed for God's service and glory. I love this book! It challenges the next generation of underdog leaders—dreamers who bring a radical approach to changing their world.

—DR. WESS STAFFORD, PRESIDENT AND CEO,
COMPASSION INTERNATIONAL

Matt is one of the most inspirational people I know. His tenacity is contagious. His insights here are universally uplifting. *God of the Underdogs* is funny, biblically grounded storytelling that is perfect for anyone who wants to experience more of God's power. Kellers' easy-to-read style will pull you in and resurrect your dreams. This is the book I want my church to read.

—PETER HAAS, LEAD PASTOR, SUBSTANCE
CHURCH; AUTHOR, *PHARISECTOMY*

I've had the incredible opportunity to experience Pastor Matt Keller's ministry up close and personal. He is, and has always been, a cheerleader for the underdog. Matt does a masterful job of pulling the rug of self-pity out from underneath you and explaining that God has always used underdogs. He challenges us to abandon the excuses and embrace the fact that it is through our weakness that God makes us strong. It will only take you a couple of chapters before you begin to realize that what you thought was a weakness may turn out to be your greatest strength, that your destiny is within reach, and that you were created for great things.

—TROY GRAMLING, LEAD PASTOR, POTENTIAL CHURCH

Everyone has felt like an underdog at some point in their life. I didn't attend college, and it's been used by some to diminish my value. Matt Keller speaks life and truth into me and you and gives us the permission to pursue God, and in doing so, to change the world.

—Tim Stevens, executive pastor, Granger Community Church; author, *Vision: Lost & Found*

I have watched Matt personally experience the God of the underdog. He has the both the credibility and ability to lead us toward the same God!

—Shawn Lovejoy, directional leader, Mountain Lake Church and Churchplanters.com; Author, *The Measure of Our Success: An Impassioned Plea to Pastors*

If you suspect that God has created you to do more than you thought you could – you must read this book! Matt Keller's **God of the Underdogs** just might cause you to recognize the excuses you have allowed to limit the great things God wants to do through you. God always asks us to do more than we could on your own but with God's help we are no longer the underdog!

—Philip Wagner, pastor, Oasis Church LA; author, *How To Turn Your Marriage Around in 10 Days*

Everyone has a dream of doing something significant with their life. But many of us find ourselves a great distance from the God-given vision we once held dear. In *God of the Underdogs*, Matt reminds us that God's vision for our lives is greater than any vision we have. The things you believe disqualify you or keep you from doing something great for God are the very things God longs to leverage in you to change the world. You can't read this book and not be challenged and encouraged to pursue your God-given purpose.

—Justin Davis, coauthor, *Beyond Ordinary: When a Good Marriage Just Isn't Good Enough*

GOD
of the
UNDERDOGS

GOD
of the
UNDERDOGS

When the Odds Are Against You,
God Is For You

MATT KELLER

NELSON
BOOKS

An Imprint of Thomas Nelson

Published in Nashville, Tennessee, by Nelson Books. Nelson Books and Thomas Nelson are registered trademarks of Thomas Nelson, Inc.

Thomas Nelson, Inc., titles may be purchased in bulk for educational, business, fund-raising, or sales promotional use. For information, please e-mail SpecialMarkets@ThomasNelson.com.

Library of Congress Cataloging-in-Publication Data

Keller, Matt, 1975-
  God of the underdogs : when the odds are against you, God is for you / Matt Keller.
    pages cm
  ISBN 978-1-4002-0496-0
  1. Failure (Psychology)--Religious aspects--Christianity 2. Success--Religious aspects--Christianity. 3. Self-perception--Religious aspects--Christianity. I. Title.
  BT730.5.G63 2013
  248.8'6--dc23

                              2013004080

Printed in the United States of America

13 14 15 16 17 RRD 6 5 4 3 2 1

To my wife, Sarah, thanks for believing and standing with this underdog. Can you believe we get to do this?

And . . . to anyone who has ever seen himself or herself as an underdog and dared to change the world anyway . . . this book is for you.

CONTENTS

CONTENTS

FOREWORD

THE UNDERDOG THEME IS ONE OF THE MOST UNIVERSALLY recognized metaphors in the world. Its imagery reaches across the centuries and crosses nationalities, race, and socioeconomic class. It is also one that I can identify with personally.

When my wife, Kay, and I moved to Southern California in December of 1979, we were underdogs. With no money, no place to live, and a four-month-old baby to take care of, we had only a U-Haul truck full of stuff, a dream, and a belief that God would use us for His purpose in starting a church in the Saddleback Valley. As you may know, that dream came true. God showed up and He used us, underdogs just like you, to grow one of the largest churches in American history and impact tens of millions of people all over the world.

Just as God used me, I am confident that He can use you too! I believe God is placing visions and dreams inside a new generation. It's exciting to see an army of young people taking their places in the world today—more than ever in this time in history. I believe in the next generation!

Let me encourage you to not just read this book but to let the message take hold of you. Matt's humor is refreshing, his storytelling is genuine, and his love for you shines through his words.

God of the Underdogs will inspire you to think about your purpose as you never have before and dream dreams you never thought possible! I believe God will use this book to ignite a passion in you to live out your purpose and change the world.

God uses underdogs. Each of us has a purpose to glorify Him with our lives and do things we never thought possible.

God bless you,

Rick Warren

Founding Pastor, Saddleback Church

Author, *The Purpose Driven Life*

INTRODUCTION
WE ARE ALL UNDERDOGS

Everyone Has an Excuse

EVERYONE LOVES AN UNDERDOG STORY. FOR AS LONG AS I can remember, I've always cheered for the underdog. Maybe it was my Chicago Cubs upbringing or the fact that I am now a die-hard Tampa Bay Rays fan. Perhaps it was being raised in a small town or being a little brother. Whether I'm watching a sporting event, a TV drama, or a movie, there is this thing inside me that pulls for the underdog. What I'm discovering is, I'm not alone. There's a little piece in all of us that wants the underdog to win.

The reason is that we are all underdogs. Deep down, we are aware of our humanity and feel that, in some way, we don't measure up. No matter where we've come from or how many accolades we've received in our lives, each one of us still sees himself or herself as an underdog.

I know I do. If I'm being honest, a lot of days I feel that the deck is stacked against me. It seems that those who are against me are more than those who are for me. That is because, in the most authentic way possible, I know myself. And in those moments when I'm face-to-face with my true self, I have to admit I'm just not that great.

All of us have that sense on certain days or in certain environments where we feel we aren't qualified to live the life we're living or do the thing we're doing. No matter how many successes have come our way or how many people follow us on social media, we are keenly aware of our humanity and shortcomings. Not just in everyday-life things but in spiritual things as well.

Perhaps when you look in the mirror you see any number of excuses why you couldn't or shouldn't be the one who accomplishes something great. Perhaps you see all the reasons why somebody else is more qualified, better looking, or more deserving.

See, we underdogs are prone to this faulty reasoning, aren't we? We have the tendency to hide behind our underdog excuses. Those logical, legitimate reasons about why it can't be done, why we're not the one, and why we ought to be disqualified. And that's the reason for this book. To look the excuses in the face and then proceed anyway!

It is time to rise up, face our underdog excuses head-on, and then get moving full speed in the direction of our dreams and our destinies. My prayer is that the stories you read in the pages of this book will inspire you to be part of a movement happening in our world today.

The days of allowing our excuses to hold us back are over. They must be. The world is poised for a new kind of leader to emerge. Not perfect leaders but underdog leaders. Men and women who understand their humanity, know the excuses that hold them back, and choose to make a difference anyway!

So listen, underdog, you're not alone. You're in really good company. Every person God chose to use in a great way in the Bible was an underdog. Every person God used had a justifiable excuse for why he or she couldn't or shouldn't be used by God to accomplish great things.

> *Everyone.*
> *No exceptions.*
> *Not one.*

Every great hero of faith in Scripture was an underdog just like you and me. Those heroes had the opportunity to let their underdog excuses hold them back, but they didn't. The stories we're going to explore will inspire you to face the excuses holding you back and pursue your destiny like never before.

If you've ever had a dream to do something great, to accomplish something significant, and to make a difference in our world but have struggled to believe you could actually do it, this book is for you. I believe you can change your world. God wants to use you as he used the greatest influencers in the Bible. You're an underdog; so were they, but they didn't let that stop them. They were individuals who overcame their excuses, served the God of the underdogs, and changed their world.

Welcome, underdog. The world is waiting for you.

Matt Keller

@MatthewKeller

UNDERDOG EXCUSE #1

"I'm Not Qualified Enough"

(DAVID)

> They asked for a king; so God gave them Saul the son
> of Kish, a man of the tribe of Benjamin, for forty years.
> And when He had removed him, He raised up for
> them David as king, to whom also He gave testimony
> and said, "I have found David the son of Jesse, a
> man after My own heart, who will do all My will."
>
> ACTS 13:21–22 NKJV

I HEARD THE BIG METAL DOOR ON THE BACK OF THE
Ryder truck slam, and the sound rang through my ears. It was six
in the morning, and it was moving day. Tightening the latch on
the back door of that truck represented the end of one chapter

of my life and the beginning of the next. To say I was scared is an understatement. After all, inside that Ryder truck was every earthly possession that Sarah and I and our eighteen-month-old son had acquired.

We knew when we crossed the Indiana state line that cold morning in January 2002, we were saying good-bye to the only home we had ever known. Until then, we had been pretty successful. For the previous three years, we had spent our days traveling and speaking in churches and at youth camps across the country. For those years we had the backing of a small fellowship of churches behind us.

But when we made the decision a few months earlier to resign as national youth director of that fellowship to pursue the dream of planting a church in Fort Myers, Florida, it wasn't received well. Leaders and mentors told us it wouldn't work. We knew we were on our own in moving to southwest Florida.

Well, not completely on our own. There was our son, still wearing diapers and learning to walk, and there were two college guys we had convinced to move with us. They liked the idea of doing ministry in a spring break town. Dave had been an intern with me for a couple of years, and the other guy, Mike—well, let's just say Mike felt a call to ministry but was definitely rough around the edges.

As for money, we weren't broke, but we were close to it. We had managed to raise $9,200 to start the new church. (We later found out that was *not* a lot of money!) Other than that, we had no jobs, no insurance, no guaranteed salary, no connections, and no clue what we were doing. In addition to feeling alone and broke, we felt unqualified for the journey ahead. I remember driving that big Ryder truck over the two days and fluctuating between exhilaration and *I think I could throw up right now* about every ten minutes.

We were scared to death. We had no idea what the future would hold; all we knew was that God had placed a dream in our hearts, and we had to obey. On January 15, 2002, we crossed the state line into Florida to begin our new life. We were underdogs. Underdogs with hearts to be used by God, but underdogs full of fear and excuses.

I'm guessing you've felt the same way at some point in your life. Perhaps it was your first day on the job or the first day of school. Maybe it was the day you brought your first child home from the hospital. (I know I was thinking the whole time, *They are really going to let us take this kid home with no more instructions or practice?*)

Maybe you were chosen to give a speech or make a presentation, and you questioned yourself the entire time. Perhaps someone actually told you that you weren't qualified. Or you made it through the first interview, but when the senior manager took one look at your resume, she called you out like an umpire ringing up strike three.

Every one of us has had those moments of feeling unqualified. That moment when we looked at what was ahead or needed in a situation and thought, *Surely I'm not the one God would want to use right now. Not this time. Not in this instance. Not me.* Human beings in every period of history have felt that way, even in Bible times.

DAVID, THE UNDERDOG

When you think of unqualified underdogs in the Bible, you have to look no further than David. David has always been a favorite Bible figure for me. I can relate to David on a lot of levels. He was a real guy with real flaws and a real heart for God and for people. I get that.

David was a guy who came from humble beginnings. He was a no-big-deal kind of kid who was thrust into the limelight in a *Price Is Right* "Come on down" TV-game-show moment. I like David because he was a world changer, but he wasn't perfect. In fact, he was a screwup in many ways. But somehow, in the midst of the multiple messes he seemed to get himself into, God still used him. God still said he was "a man after My own heart" (Acts 13:22 NKJV).

King David changed the world. He took his nation in a whole new direction and changed the face of the world from that time on. Jesus was a descendant of David. Forty-two generations after David came Jesus. And Jesus changed the world as well. But here's the thing about David. Long before he changed the world, led his nation in a new direction, and became Jesus' ancestor, he was a whole lot of nothing special. Actually, that's probably still overstating it a bit. See, when we first meet David, he's anything *but* a world changer and a king. When we first meet David, he is an underdog. First Samuel 16 tells us the story.

THE FIRST KING: SAUL

In ancient Israel, a few centuries before Jesus came on the scene, God's people started grumbling about wanting a king. Until that point, God had been their King. He spoke and led them, and it had worked out fine. Except for one small detail: they couldn't see him. So over an extended period of time they began asking for a king they could see. They wanted to be able to see and feel and touch the king leading them, not just hear from him or about him.

However, God, knowing what was best for them, was like, "Trust me. You don't want that. An earthly king will only mess things up. I'll be your King. Trust me. It's just better that way." Well, they didn't receive that, so they kept going back and forth with God about it. After much debate, God relented and basically told them, "Okay, fine, have it your way," and he gave them a king whose name was Saul.

Now, here's what you need to know about this first king, Saul: he was, by earthly standards, the ultimate king. He looked more like a linebacker than a king. The Bible tells us he stood a head taller than everybody else in the land. He was big and strong and happened to be a fierce warrior. By outward appearances, Saul was the man.

So Saul became the first king over the children of Israel. And for a while things were okay. The children of Israel were happy, Saul was happy, and everybody won—except that Saul started getting a bit schizophrenic in his leadership style. God spoke to Saul, and one minute he was cool with it, and the next minute he was doing his own thing and rejecting God's way.

This went on for quite a while. Saul went back and forth between wanting to please God and wanting to do his own thing. Back and forth, back and forth, like a tennis match. Obviously, this situation didn't make God very happy. So eventually, God decided his patience with Saul had run out, and he announced he was lifting his hand of anointing off Saul. God decided to go in a whole new direction and would choose a new leader for his people.

CUT TO THE PRESENT DAY

I believe we're living in a similar time. Unfortunately, our world is filled with one headline after another of leaders who have gotten a bit schizophrenic in their leadership. From political figures having affairs to corporate executives embezzling and cheating loyal employees out of millions of dollars, the world we now live in has chosen its own way over God's way and, consequently, has lost its way.

And sadly, the body of Christ is no exception. Not a month goes by that we don't read of yet another leader in the body of Christ who has decided to choose his own way over God's best way. *Scandals, affairs,* and *embezzlement* are terms used to describe far too many church leaders' actions today.

That was the case in ancient Israel with Saul, and that is the case today. But just as God stepped in to change a nation's course, so I believe God is stepping in once again to our world to change its course. God is doing a new thing in our world today. In the same way God moved in a new direction after Saul, God is moving in a new direction today.

He is looking for men and women willing to be a part of a new group of underdogs. And the first and loudest message you must get from this book is that you have permission to believe

God wants to use you. Let me repeat that because I don't want you to miss it:

YOU HAVE PERMISSION TO BELIEVE
GOD WANTS TO USE YOU.

Now, here's what I realize: right about now, you're probably thinking, *Yeah, sure, Matt, I believe that on some level, but come on, it's probably* not *me.* If you're thinking that, trust me. I understand. It's easy to dismiss the possibility that God might actually be calling us to lead and change our world. It's easy to see ourselves as underdogs.

But what if? What if it's true? What if it's possible God might want to take our world in a new direction? And what if he might place his hand on a bunch of underdogs just like you and me to do it? If that's true, think of the implications. Imagine what could be possible if a movement of underdogs across our world began to rise up and take our world in a new direction!

Imagine the life change that could take place. Imagine the problems we could solve. Imagine the impact we could make. Imagine the pains and injustices plaguing so many in our world today that we could alleviate if we, the underdogs, actually gave ourselves permission to believe we are the ones God wants to use.

MY PERSONAL STORY

Long before Sarah and I moved to southwest Florida to start Next Level Church, I wrestled with the kind of permission we're talking about. I began my relationship with Jesus Christ at the age of fifteen and felt a call to give my entire life to ministry the following summer right after I turned sixteen years old. I was inexperienced and naïve, but I knew God had called me to give my life to lead in my generation.

At the same summer camp a few years later, I felt that God gave me my life verse. I was kneeling in front of a chair during a worship time one night, and I sensed God telling me to open my Bible and read 2 Timothy 2:10. I reached down under my chair, pulled out my Bible, and turned there. When I read it, I sensed God speaking to my heart that this verse would become the foundation for the calling of my life.

When I read the verse, I instantly knew this was true. The verse says, "Therefore I endure everything for the sake of the elect, that they too may obtain the salvation that is in Christ Jesus, with eternal glory" (NIV). I knew the elect that Paul spoke of in this verse, for my life, was my generation. That hot summer night in a campground church service, I knew God was calling me, a kid from small-town America, to endure anything and everything so my generation could obtain salvation in Jesus Christ and impact the world for eternal glory. That night I received my calling as an underdog.

THE REASON YOU'RE HOLDING
THIS BOOK IN YOUR HANDS

That's why you're holding this book in your hands right now. Because a long time ago God placed his hand on me, an underdog, and put a vision in my heart to inspire a group of underdogs to rise up and take the church of Jesus Christ and the world in a new direction. The world needs us. This is our time.

As you will see in the next few pages, God's not looking at outward qualifiers; he's looking at the heart. God's not looking for the obvious choice; he's looking for you. Believe it. You are the one God wants to use to change the world and, specifically, your world. God's into the whole underdog thing. God's into the unexpected. And David just happened to be an unexpected underdog.

> God's not looking for the obvious choice; he's looking for you.

BACK TO 1 SAMUEL 16

In the old days of the Bible, when God wanted to choose a king, he would speak to the prophet to anoint a new king. That meant the prophet was supposed to get a big bucket of oil and pour it on the new king. (I know it sounds like a crazy idea, but it's how they did it.)

So, in 1 Samuel 16, God had rejected Saul and was ready to anoint a new king, but Samuel, the prophet, wasn't so hip on the idea. After all, he had been a major player in getting the earthly king idea rolling for the children of Israel, so to hear God was breaking his end of the bargain made Samuel pretty upset. It's like being a real estate agent who puts together a multimillion-dollar deal and on the last day before the contract expires, one of the parties bails out. You've done all the hard work, and now it's disintegrating right before your eyes.

Samuel was moping around big-time. He was probably wearing pajama pants around the house and eating chips on the couch. There's a good chance he hadn't showered in a while. That's when God spoke to him. "The LORD said to Samuel, 'How long will you mourn for Saul, since I have rejected him as king over Israel?'" (1 Sam. 16:1 NIV).

God was saying, "Hey, Samuel, you've moped around long enough. I'm ready to move on, and I need you to help me. We need to anoint a new king, so get up off the couch, take a shower, and let's get going." But notice Samuel's hesitation: "Samuel said, 'How can I go? If Saul hears about it, he will kill me'" (1 Sam. 16:2 NIV).

I love Samuel's reply to God. To paraphrase: "Um, God, love the idea. Thanks for the prompting, but if you haven't noticed, here's the deal: we already have a king! And I don't need to remind you that he's built like a linebacker! Great idea, God. Our present king is the best warrior our nation has ever seen. So as much as I appreciate being included in the new deal, when Saul hears about it, he's probably going to want to kill somebody. And if given the choice between killing you, an unseen God, and killing me, a mere mortal, I'm betting he will probably kill me! So thanks, but no thanks!"

Personally, I think Samuel's logic was solid. But God didn't even flinch. "The LORD said, 'Take a heifer with you and say, "I have come to sacrifice to the LORD"'" (1 Sam. 16:2 NIV).

God totally blew off Samuel's excuse and was like, "Samuel, zip it. Go get the cow and get moving." Then he gave Samuel very specific instructions on how to find this new king. He told Samuel to go to a little town called Bethlehem and get everybody together. But he was to make sure one family in particular was represented at the church service. God said, "Invite Jesse to the sacrifice, and

I will show you what to do. You are to anoint for me the one I indicate" (1 Sam. 16:3 NIV).

God told Samuel to make sure some guy named Jesse had his family there, and then at that point, stay tuned because he would tell him whom to choose. God had a plan for the direction he wanted the world to go, and he needed Samuel to listen and obey.

NO TIME FOR FEAR

What God wants to do in our world isn't fuzzy in his mind. It is crystal clear. It's easy for those of us living in this day and age to get freaked out by all the craziness happening around us, isn't it? But we must know this: God is not freaked out by any of it. God is raising up leaders, and one of those leaders is you. Regardless of how much of an underdog you may think you are, God wants to use you to do a new thing on the earth today!

If we're waiting for all the stars to align before we step out for God, we're going to miss it. If we're waiting for the economy to be better, we're going to miss it. There's no time to hesitate. Samuel hesitated. We must not. God is choosing new underdogs, and the ones he chooses just might surprise you.

DOWN TO BETHLEHEM

After a quick shower, Samuel went down to Bethlehem and announced a church service for that night. He probably rounded up an organist, a pulpit, and a choir, and then he found Jesse and slipped him some special front-row tickets in the VIP section for the whole family. Can't you see Jesse running home, going, "Honey, get the boys. We're going to church"?

A few hours later Samuel and the whole town gathered under the big tent, and the church service started. Mildred, the organist, was probably squinting to see hymn #23 through her Coke-bottle glasses, and the choir was step-touching on the left side of the platform. Jesse and the boys were right there on the first row. After they sang four songs, listened to three announcements, and heard Samuel preach his inspirational message, it was finally time for the anointing service.

At that point, Samuel had Jesse and the boys stand up in the VIP section, and he pointed to the oldest son, Eliab. When Samuel saw Eliab, he immediately started making assumptions. Eliab was tall, dark, and handsome. In the right light, he looked a bit like Saul, as a matter of fact. So Samuel naturally assumed he must be the guy. Samuel assumed he knew what God wanted to do. "When they arrived, Samuel saw Eliab and thought, 'Surely the LORD's anointed stands here before the LORD'" (1 Sam. 16:6 NIV).

But God shut him down immediately. "The LORD said to Samuel, 'Do not consider his appearance or his height, for I have rejected him. The LORD does not look at the things people look at. People look at the outward appearance, but the LORD looks at the heart'" (1 Sam. 16:7 NIV).

Bam! God put the smackdown on Samuel. He wanted him to know that this new thing was going to look different. "Hey, Samuel, don't assume you know what he's supposed to look like."

SAME MESSAGE, NEW PACKAGE

When we moved to southwest Florida in 2002 to start the church, we knew it would have to look different from anything we had ever seen. We were looking for a new way to present the message of Jesus Christ. Same message, new package. If we were going to be effective, our church would have to look different.

The same is true in our world today. God is raising up a new breed of underdogs with visions that don't fit the old model. If your dream doesn't look like anything you've ever seen, don't count it out; it just might be from God. The vision God has placed in your heart might not fit in the box that you've seen used before. That's okay. God is placing dreams and visions in the hearts of underdogs that have the power to change the world.

THE SECOND SON

After God rebuked Samuel about assuming whom he would choose as the new king, Jesse called the second son. "Then Jesse called Abinadab and had him pass in front of Samuel. But Samuel said, 'The Lord has not chosen this one either'" (1 Sam. 16:8 NIV).

He wasn't the guy either. Then Shammah, the third in line, stood up. And God was like, "Um, yeah, hate to tell you this, but it's not him either." "Jesse then had Shammah pass by, but Samuel said, 'Nor has the Lord chosen this one'" (1 Sam. 16:9 NIV).

Seven times that happened. Seven sons stood up; seven sons

sat down. Rejected. God didn't choose any of the ones whom society would have deemed right for the job. Apparently, God had a different plan.

AWKWARD MOMENTS ALL OVER THE PLACE

Can you imagine being there? I mean, seriously, put yourself in the story. You and the spouse are sitting about eight rows back, and the first son goes by. When you see him stand up, you whisper, "Oh, I just love Eliab." But then Samuel rejects him. You think it is a little harsh, but it's all good, right? There's still a whole row of sons to choose from. Then the next one gets shot down. And the next one. And the next one. At some point, you start thinking, *Man, this is really depressing.* But if being in the audience is awkward, imagine being one of the brothers!

Imagine being number six in line when Eliab's name is called. You'd be thinking, *Man, Eliab always gets to do the fun stuff.* And then when he's rejected, you're like, *What's up now, Eliab?* Then Abinadab goes by, and you're thinking, *They didn't choose him either.* Samuel makes it all the way down to you, and you get rejected too. That's a humiliating day!

Now, imagine being Samuel. Not only do you have to let a half-dozen brothers down easy, but then, after all the sons have paraded by, Samuel has to do the most awkward thing ever: he asks Jesse if he has any other kids. "So he asked Jesse, 'Are these all the sons you have?'" (1 Sam. 16:11 NIV).

"I don't mean to insult you, but any chance you forgot any of your kids?" As a pastor, I can relate to this. That would be the same as me asking the nice new family in the foyer of our church if by any chance they left any of their kids back in our Kids' Zone! Awkward.

But then it goes from bad to worse. "'There is still the youngest,' Jesse answered. 'He is tending the sheep'" (1 Sam. 16:11 NIV).

Jesse actually admitted he left out one of his kids! "Oh my goodness, thanks for reminding me. Actually, I did forget one! See, little Davey doesn't represent our family very well, so we thought we'd just leave him out in the field by himself!" Jesse won the worst-dad-in-the-world award hands down that night. I mean, really, how do you forget a kid, for crying out loud? But he did, and it wasn't an accident.

Jesse didn't think David mattered. Why bring him in from the field for the ceremony? It was not like it was ever going to get to him anyway. Seriously, have you seen the older sons? They're all way more qualified and more capable than he is. No point calling him in from caring for the sheep?

By not inviting him to the ceremony in the first place, it was as if Jesse, David's father, was saying, "Why bother? David's just the runt. He's the baby of the family. He's just a shepherd. He's small and scrawny. He's unqualified. Surely God couldn't want to use an unqualified afterthought underdog like David, right?" David's father didn't see or believe in David's potential.

FEELING LIKE THE UNDERDOG

Maybe you're reading this and somewhere in your past someone hasn't believed in you. Maybe it was a parent or a teacher. Maybe it was a coach, a boss, a sibling, or a friend. Maybe it's been your own voice that's told you that you weren't good enough. Perhaps that unbelief has become an excuse that has held you back from pursuing your God-given destiny. If that's you, you need to know you are no different from David.

Yes, that David! The same King David who ruled Israel and changed history began his journey as an underdog with low expectations. The same King David whose father didn't think enough of him to invite him to the anointing ceremony.

If you know the kind of pain someone's unbelief can cause, you must hear me right now: God knows who you are, where you are, and when you are. You are not a mistake. You are chosen of God to break the curse of unbelief on you!

YOU HAVE PERMISSION TO BREAK THE
CURSE AND BEGIN ANEW TODAY.

What happened next was powerful and telling. It was more than a side note. After Jesse confessed his bad-dad moment, Samuel made a statement that was completely opposite of the one David's father just made. "Samuel said, 'Send for him; we will not sit down until he arrives'" (1 Sam. 16:11 NIV).

Standing when someone enters a room is a symbol of respect we still use and value today. The moment Samuel learned of David's existence, he began treating him as royalty. By making everyone stand until David arrived, Samuel was communicating to the crowd that they were going to be in the presence of royalty. Quite different from his dad just a minute before, wasn't it? One leader in David's life saw his potential; one did not. And that belief made all the difference.

16

IN THE PRESENCE OF SOMEONE
WHO BELIEVES IN YOU

I don't know what voices have spoken over you in your past, but my prayer since I began writing this book has been for God to break the power of those voices in your life. I believe that you, the underdog reader, will see yourself differently from now on. I pray the words you read in the pages of this book will awaken inside you a belief you've never had before. Just like David, you have the potential to change the world and change *your* world. I believe that, and I believe in you.

ENTER DAVID, THE UNDERDOG

"So he sent for him and had him brought in. He was glowing with health and had a fine appearance and handsome features. Then the Lord said, 'Rise and anoint him; he is the one'" (1 Sam. 16:12 NIV).

God chose David to be the one to lead, and nobody saw it coming. Nobody would have guessed it. He was a shepherd boy, for crying out loud. He was a nobody, a runt. He was a half-pint, a pip-squeak. He wasn't famous, nor was he raised in the right family or even in the right birth order. Everything that could have been wrong with David was, except that God chose him. David was the unexpected underdog.

Maybe you've looked at yourself and thought, *I'm not good enough or qualified enough. I graduated in the bottom half of my class (or didn't graduate at all).* Maybe you've always told yourself that you're not as pretty as your sister, or you didn't go to the right university. Maybe your parents weren't proud of you. If so, this next statement is for you:

ALL THE WRONG STUFF, PLUS GOD'S HAND OF
ANOINTING, EQUALS THE RIGHT PERSON FOR THE JOB.

You have permission to believe you are God's right person for the job. It's you. You are the one God wants to use. I believe God has placed a vision inside your heart, and he is calling you to rise up and make it happen.

What God wants to do in our world will require every one of us, a new breed of underdogs, to courageously pursue our dreams and change our world. A world full of hurting, broken, desperate people is out there, and we've got the answer. People are wandering aimlessly, pursuing everything from fame and money to position and power. They are searching for what we have to offer. God is calling us, the underdogs, to rise up with the message of hope in Jesus Christ that has the power to change their world.

DAVID'S VERY NEXT ACT

Interestingly enough, the very next event the Bible records in the life of David included a giant named Goliath. In the next chapter of 1 Samuel, David went to the battlefield to deliver some sandwiches to his brothers and came home a hero. How was that possible? How could a scrawny, teenage shepherd boy go from nobody to giant slayer in one chapter? The answer is belief.

David slew Goliath that day because he was armed with more than a slingshot and five smooth stones. He was armed with the power that comes from knowing God's hand was on him. With that knowledge, David changed the destiny of a nation and the world. For the next forty-plus years, David led the nation of Israel in a direction that brought unprecedented blessing and prosperity upon them.

We will talk more about David's life in chapter 6, but suffice it to say, he changed his world. David lived one of the most historic and storied lives of any leader in the history of the world. Though not perfect, David honored God, lived courageously, and led the nation of Israel in a magnificent direction that ultimately set the stage for Jesus—his great-great-grandson generations later—to change the world forever. David overcame his underdog excuse of not feeling qualified enough and changed the world anyway.

A NEW BREED OF UNDERDOGS NEEDED

Saul didn't get the job done. So God called a new underdog, David. The same call goes out to you. Today, you are receiving your calling to be an underdog God uses to impact the world. You have permission to believe that it's you. You're the one God is waiting to use to make a difference in your world.

Today, God wants to set you free from past condemnation, from past words spoken over you, from past sin. God wants to set you free to rise up and change your world. God is giving you the courage to be the leader he's called you to be. God has placed his hand on you, just as he did with David, and he is choosing you, the unexpected underdog, to change the world.

TheUnderdogsBook.com/ch1

SCAN HERE FOR BONUS CONTENT ABOUT "LIVING UP TO YOUR POTENTIAL."

2

UNDERDOG EXCUSE #2

"My Past Is Too Bad"
(PAUL)

> { Now get up and stand on your feet.
> ACTS 26:16 NIV }

TO SAY THE FIRST TWO YEARS OF PLANTING NEXT LEVEL
Church were difficult would be understating it. Looking back,
they were, hands down, the two most difficult years of my life.
Prior to moving to southwest Florida, Sarah and I had a pretty
high-profile position in our small fellowship of churches in the
Midwest. We were big fish in a small pond. I became a national
youth director at the age of twenty-three, which meant we spent
forty-five weeks a year traveling all over the country speaking in

21

churches, hosting youth conferences and camps, and building awareness for the next generation.

As I mentioned earlier, when we moved to Florida, we had $9,200 to our name, two college guys, and no clue what we were doing. To make matters worse, we felt forgotten by many leaders who had influenced us before we moved. Men who had been mentors to me never called—that type of thing. It was a dark and painful season, to say the least. We were dealing with personal hurt and rejection and trying to get our little church plant off the ground.

I remember so many Sunday mornings standing at the doors of our rented movie theater knocking until my knuckles were bruised (literally) in an attempt to get the night cleaning crew's attention so they would come and let us in so we could set up church. In those days, we were the set-up crew, the trailer haulers, the worship team, the greeters, the ushers, the announcement makers, the preacher, the offering-taker-uppers, and the tear-down crew. We did all that before noon when the theater needed us out! It was hard work. We were lonely and clueless. The first two years were some of the darkest of our entire past. Our little church plant was an underdog. We were underdogs. Underdogs with a dark, hurt-filled, and painful past.

DIFFERENT KIND OF DARK

There's a guy in the Bible who had a pretty dark past as well, but in a different kind of way. His dark past was one that should have disqualified him from ever being used by God to do anything great. And yet the apostle Paul was the person God used to write two-thirds of the New Testament. His words continue to be the vehicle God uses to impact billions of people. Paul was an underdog with a past different from mine, but a past nonetheless. A past that threatened to disqualify him.

In Acts 26, we hear the apostle Paul describe his past in his own words. Let me set the scenario for you. Paul was summoned to meet with a big-dog official in the government, King Agrippa. The reason for the meeting centered on Paul's preaching of the message that changed his life, the message of Jesus Christ. Paul had been preaching all over the nation, and his message was polarizing people, especially religious people, left and right. Finally, the religious leaders of the day were able to apprehend him and take him before King Agrippa.

What ensued in Acts 26 was Paul answering questions about the past that should have disqualified him. After some pleasantries with the big dog, Paul began to describe himself in his former life, and we begin to see just how messed up his past really was:

> *The Jewish people all know the way I have lived ever since I was a child, from the beginning of my life in my own country, and also in Jerusalem. They have known me for a long time and can testify, if they are willing, that I conformed to the strictest sect of our religion, living as a Pharisee. (Acts 26:4–5 NIV)*

Paul identified himself as a member of one of the most self-righteous, arrogant groups of religious leaders anywhere in his day. Paul boldly spoke of his dependence on his own abilities and skills. Not only was he arrogant, but he was a bit of a punk too:

"I too was convinced that I ought to do all that was possible to oppose the name of Jesus of Nazareth" (Acts 26:9 NIV).

Paul was not just self-reliant and arrogant; he actually worked aggressively against anyone who named the name of Jesus! He said, "On the authority of the chief priests I put many of the Lord's people in prison, and when they were put to death, I cast my vote against them" (Acts 26:10 NIV).

Did you catch that? Paul had Christians put to death! But he didn't stop there: "Many a time I went from one synagogue to another to have them punished, and I tried to force them to blaspheme. I was so obsessed with persecuting them that I even hunted them down in foreign cities" (Acts 26:11 NIV).

Paul, in his own words, admitted that he was "obsessed" with persecuting, torturing, and killing Christians. If ever there was a guy whose past was too bad to be used by God, he was it. Paul's past made him an underdog—one seriously dark and messed-up underdog.

WHAT'S IN YOUR PAST?

For a long time, I resented the fact that I didn't have a horrible, dark, drug-infested past like many of the stories I heard in the church world as I was growing up. I actually went through a season when I prayed that God would give me a "past." I suppose I wanted to be able to relate to people in that situation, or maybe I just thought it would be a better story.

However, through the years, I've learned that even a non-past is still a past. Every story has dark seasons and dark

UNDERDOG EXCUSE #2

moments. For Paul, they included murder and evildoing. For me, they have looked completely different. Everyone whom God wants to use greatly, he first tests greatly. Don't resent your story if it's not super dark. Be thankful for it. God uses every past that is yielded to him.

Maybe when you look over your past, you're tempted to think it has the power to disqualify you from being able to be used by God. Maybe you review entire chapters of your life story and categorize them as "dark." Maybe you're ashamed of decisions you've made, consequences you've suffered, and even people you've wounded or hurt.

Maybe you've lived with regret and pain because of your past. Just about the time you begin to move forward in your life, your past creeps up behind you and sabotages your confidence. Maybe you've found yourself paralyzed in your relationships, your finances, or even your relationship with God because of the darkness of your past. If so, you must hear this: if we can learn anything from the life of Paul, it's that there's no past too dark that it will disqualify someone from being used in the present and the future.

One of the greatest enemies to our future is our past.

The truth is, we've all got a past. Some are darker than others, but we all have one. Some can relate to the sin-filled past of someone like Paul, while others may have been victims of abuse or broken trust that was no fault of their own. Regardless of what forms our pasts take, they're not too big or too dark to disqualify us from being used by God in the future.

One of the greatest enemies to our future is our past. We

must learn to overcome the stuff of our past, or it will always hold power over us. If you and I don't learn how to overcome it and leverage it, it has the potential of becoming the lid to what God can do through us in the future. Just as our past has the power to hold us captive, so the opposite is true. The enemy of our souls wants to use our past to hold us back, but God intends to use it to influence others for his glory!

LEARNING TO LEVERAGE OUR PAST

During chapter 26, Paul turned a corner in his testifying to King Agrippa. He moved from clarifying his past to declaring his present and future. In the next few verses Paul gave us the secret to unlocking our past's hold on us and leveraging it for the future:

> On one of these journeys I was going to Damascus with the authority and commission of the chief priests. About noon, King Agrippa, as I was on the road, I saw a light from heaven, brighter than the sun, blazing around me and my companions. We all fell to the ground, and I heard a voice saying to me in Aramaic, "Saul, Saul, why do you persecute me? It is hard for you to kick against the goads." (Acts 26:12–14 NIV)

Basically, Paul was on another mission to destroy more Christians when he had a life-altering moment. He was knocked off his high horse by a powerful light. From the light he heard a voice. Perplexed by the voice, Paul dared to ask who was speaking to him: "'Who are you, Lord?' 'I am Jesus, whom you are persecuting'" (Acts 26:15 NIV).

Boom! Hammer dropped! It was the voice of Jesus. The one he had been so violently opposing. In that moment, lying in the dirt on the road, Paul had a life-changing encounter.

Overcoming our past begins with a life-altering moment: a moment when we realize that how we've been living isn't pleasing to God. For Paul (then known as Saul; God changed his name later), it was this moment on the Damascus road. He was instantly brought face-to-face with the darkness in his life, and he was rocked to the core. Paul's life was never the same after that moment.

MY ENCOUNTER MOMENT

When I was fifteen years old I had a moment like Paul had. Now, you're probably thinking, *Seriously, Keller, how dark can your past be at the age of fifteen?* And if you're thinking that, you're right. Honestly, I was a good kid growing up. I never drank or did drugs. I never got into a lot of the trouble that my friends did. I was raised in a good home with morally upstanding parents who loved us, gave us great opportunities, took us on vacations, and tried to teach us to be good people.

But at the age of fifteen, something changed for me. I was invited to an Easter musical at the church of a girl I liked. Over that hour and a half, I saw the gospel story play out right in front of me, complete with Jesus dying on the cross and being resurrected from the dead. It really had an impact on me! At the end, the pastor gave a simple invitation to everyone in the audience to "accept Jesus as Lord and Savior."

Growing up in a traditional church, I had never experienced anything like that before, so I knew instantly I wanted to raise my hand. That Friday night of Easter weekend in 1991 changed my life forever. In that moment, I knew I no longer wanted to just be a good person. I knew I wanted to serve God with my whole life. That Friday night became the first of what would become several encounter moments that changed my life forever.

MORE ENCOUNTER MOMENTS

I started going to the youth group on Wednesday nights after the Easter program. (Oh yeah, I eventually married the girl who invited me that night.) The following summer I went with the youth group to summer camp, and on one Tuesday night, I had another encounter moment with Jesus.

When the guest speaker ended his message, he gave an opportunity for people who felt God might be calling them into full-time ministry to step out of their seats and come forward for prayer. And in that moment, I had another one of those Paul-type encounter moments. Honestly, it wasn't like the sky opened up or the roof flew open with a heavenly light; it was just a confident knowing that God didn't want me to be an architect or a psychiatrist (which was what I thought I wanted to be till then), but that God wanted me to be a pastor and a leader in my generation.

I could tell story after story about a dozen of these types of moments when I had a life-changing encounter with God that altered the course of my life forever. I don't know what that will look like for you, but I know the first step in overcoming your past and leveraging it for your future is found in having a God encounter of your own.

If you've never experienced something like that, I strongly encourage you to get alone with God sometime soon and seek him in a way that will transform you. The Bible makes it clear that God is a rewarder of those who diligently seek him. That means if you seek him, you'll find him.

This happened for Mike Ash, one of the guys who helped us plant the church and is now one of my best friends. About a year after we moved to Florida, I remember Mike wrestling with a few things in his past that were holding him captive. So I encouraged him to take a road trip for a couple of days, get alone with God, and allow God to turn his past into something he could leverage for his future. I'll never forget him returning and describing what happened. That was the first of several God encounters Mike has had over the last decade. Overcoming your past begins with an encounter moment.

Today, Mike continues to serve on our church staff. In fact, he is the boss! Only one guy in the organizational flowchart reports to me, and that's Mike. He oversees our entire staff of more than thirty people and is ultimately responsible for leading hundreds of volunteers throughout our organization. Mike has grown into one of the strongest and most talented leaders I know. God is using his life to change the lives of so many people and leaders across the country today. But Mike would not be doing what he is doing if it weren't for several encounter moments, like the one I just described, along the way.

ONE MOMENT CAN CHANGE YOUR LIFE

An encounter moment will look different for everyone. For some it's a conversation they need to have. Someone else may need to seek out a counselor to talk through issues from the past. It might be the moment when a dad decides to go home instead of staying at the office late into the evening every night of the week. Or the moment when a college student makes the decision to stop sleeping with a different girl every weekend. Perhaps it is the decision to stop overeating and start exercising. One moment can change your life forever.

It's the moment when we decide, *Enough is enough!* The moment when we determine that the way we've been living isn't working anymore. Paul had a powerful encounter with Jesus Christ that changed the trajectory of his life forever. And God wants no different for you, underdog! You will never realize the future God has planned for you until you have a powerful encounter with God that changes everything! It's time to stop living under the weight of your past and be changed by a God encounter. Make a decision right now to get alone with God in the next few days or weeks and create space for God to change you forever.

YOU CAN'T KEEP A BAD MAN DOWN

Getting back to Paul's account before King Agrippa, I love what happens next in the story. After Jesus got Paul's attention, look what Jesus said to him: "Now get up and stand on your feet" (Acts 26:16 NIV).

After getting Paul's attention, the first thing Jesus said to him was, "Get up!" In other words, *Yeah, I had to knock you down. Yes, your past has taken you off your feet, but I don't want you to live that way.* One of the biggest tools Satan will use against you concerning your past is condemnation. Condemnation from your past will tie your hands if you let it. So many underdogs are suffocating under its weight. It is killing their dreams. It's killing their present, and it's killing their future.

Jesus wanted Paul to know there was no room and no time for condemnation to rule his life. And remember, Paul had one dark past. He *killed* followers of Jesus! Now Jesus was communicating to Paul to get up and stand on his feet. Jesus was telling Paul that he was not condemned, and his living under condemnation would not be pleasing to God.

The religious world of Paul's day thrived on condemnation and guilt. When someone made a mistake, they loved to point him out as the sinner, degrade him, and make him live under the weight of that condemnation for a long, long time.

Unfortunately, the world we live in, both inside and outside the church, loves to do the same. Our world loves to capitalize on guilt and condemnation. Our world loves to find someone who's more messed up than it is, and then blow that horn as loud and for as long as it possibly can. (Think Hollywood celebrities.) Many TV shows and websites generate millions of dollars of revenue making sure the world knows how the latest celebrity or leader has tarnished his or her life. Their entire aim is to make sure no one can forget it anytime soon. In my opinion, the scrutiny of the media in our world today is keeping some of the best leaders in my generation from serving our nation simply because they don't want to put their families and themselves through that kind of wringer.

If we're ever going to overcome our past and leverage it for our future, we must be willing to let go of condemnation and guilt that try to keep us down. Jesus' first declaration to Paul had to do with condemnation. If Jesus didn't want Paul to live under that weight, surely he doesn't want us to live under it either.

What condemning voices are you living under in your life? What voice rings loud in your ear anytime you start to step out and live your underdog dream? Maybe it's a parent who told you that you'd never amount to anything. Maybe it's a teacher or a coach who told you that you were a failure. Maybe it's your own voice that keeps shouting that you don't deserve an opportunity opened to you. We must silence the voices that want to point to our dark pasts more than to our bright futures. When we do that, we take a giant step toward overcoming our past and leveraging it for our future.

Here's the good news: the more you and I silence the condemning voices, the easier it gets. Not that they ever go away completely, but with time and practice, the voices in our heads that condemn us will eventually grow quieter and quieter. The key is to replace the condemning messages with truth: the truth of who Jesus says we are.

WHO ARE WE, ACCORDING TO JESUS?

Jesus told Paul to "get up and stand on your feet." Then the very next thing he said was, "I have appeared to you" (Acts 26:16 NIV). When Paul saw who Jesus was and who he was in light of Jesus, condemnation took off like a two-year-old at Walmart whose mom lets him out of the cart.

The most powerful way to silence the voices of condemnation in our lives is to replace them with truths from God's Word about who we really are, according to Jesus. I challenge you to do a word study in the New Testament of the words *you are*. I did this several years ago, and my life has never been the same. When we discover who Jesus says we are, those words become more powerful than the condemning voices of our past.

When we study the New Testament, we discover that among other things, the Bible says we are

- friends of God
- beloved
- precious
- highly esteemed
- known
- more than conquerors

The list goes on and on. The more we know about who Jesus says we are, the less we'll believe who our past says we are. The more light we let in, the less darkness can stay.

APPOINTED AND CHOSEN

After Jesus told Paul to get up and stand on his feet, he made another powerful statement that gives us yet another key to overcoming our past and leveraging it for our future: "Now get up and stand on your feet. I have appeared to you to appoint you as a servant and as a witness of what you have seen and will see of me" (Acts 26:16 NIV).

Jesus told Paul that he had appointed him to something great. Jesus intended to take this underdog with a dark past and use him as a servant and a witness to a group of people who never would hear the gospel otherwise. Don't miss this. I believe this could be one of the greatest truths of this entire book. Paul's pain and past became his platform. Let me say that again:

PAUL'S PAIN AND PAST BECAME HIS PLATFORM.

Jesus' intention was not just to forgive Paul of his past and release him from the condemnation of it; his intention was to leverage it to impact others. It was precisely because Paul had experienced all he had in his past that positioned him to be used so powerfully in the future. Don't read that too quickly. Paul's past positioned him to be used by God in the future.

THE DARK YEARS OF NEXT LEVEL CHURCH

As I mentioned at the outset of this chapter, the first two years of planting Next Level Church were by far the darkest and most painful years of my life. We felt so lonely, so clueless, and so hurt by the leaders who we felt had abandoned us that it would have been easy for that hurt to make us jaded moving forward. But in those early dark days, Sarah and I made a decision that has shaped our ministry and leadership.

I remember sitting on the side of our bed in our little two-bedroom apartment on the wrong side of town and feeling so lonely, hurt, and broken. I remember in the midst of the pain saying to my wife, "We have a choice to make: either we can become bitter, or we can decide

> Our pain and our past have become our platform.

to become teachable." That night we cried and prayed together and made a decision. I remember saying to her, "If God lets us live through this, we will spend the rest of our lives making sure no one ever has to feel the way we feel right now."

That night we dedicated ourselves to spending our lives loving and investing in other leaders, pastors, and church planters. That decision has become the foundation of our lives. We have dedicated ourselves to investing in leaders who think that no one else truly believes in them. That is why we are passionate about coaching, training, and leading leaders. The passion of our lives is to inspire a generation to become everything God has destined for them to become. And that vision was birthed in a season of darkness, heartache, and pain.

Our pain and our past have become our platform. And we wouldn't trade it for the world. Was it dark? Yes. Was it painful? Yes. But now that it's yielded to Jesus, it has become the platform that gives us the authority to lead, speak, write, and inspire a generation.

THE SAME CAN BE TRUE FOR YOU

If God can do that for Paul and he can do that for me, I know he can do that for you as well! God wants to use the pain, the brokenness, and the darkness of your past as the platform for your future. Your past has the potential to become your greatest platform if you'll allow Jesus to take it, transform it, and leverage it for his glory.

Some of you reading this right now need to stop cursing your past. You are so busy being angry at your regrets and mistakes that you're forfeiting the power in them to be transforming agents of the Spirit in the lives of others. You need to stop minimizing your past or trying to pretend it doesn't exist or didn't happen.

Minimized pain is pain that still has control over you.

What happened cannot be changed, but what you choose to do with it can. A minimized past is a minimized platform. Minimized pain is pain that still has control over you. Stop minimizing, and start surrendering your past to Jesus. He can do far more with your past than you can cover up or minimize. He wants to take your past and make something great from it. That's his specialty.

When you study the life and teachings of the apostle Paul, you discover he never bragged about his past, but he never minimized it or denied it either. He surrendered it to Jesus and then used it as a testimony of what God can do. God wants to do the same for you. Your past is part of what makes you an underdog through whom God wants to do big things.

We've all been given different pasts for a reason. My past won't look like yours, and yours isn't going to be like anybody else's. But that's on purpose. God needs all underdogs to own our past because when we do, we present the most magnificent picture of the grace of God to our world. When we do, the results will blow our minds.

THE RESULTS

Jesus told Paul why he was rescuing him and changing his dark past:

> *I am sending you to them [the unbelieving world, known as the Gentiles] to open their eyes and turn them from darkness to light, and from the power of Satan to God, so that they may receive forgiveness of sins and a place among those who are sanctified by faith in me. (Acts 26:17–18 NIV)*

Jesus wanted to leverage Paul's past so that others' eyes could be opened. Your story, too, has the power to open people's eyes to Jesus like nothing else could for them. The unique pieces of your story that make it yours are the very things God will use to open others' eyes to see a side of Jesus they never knew existed. Jesus told Paul that his past had the power to turn people from darkness to light. How ironic that one person's darkness, when yielded to God, can bring light into someone else's darkness!

When it comes to the story of our church plant, the painful parts are the most encouraging to leaders across the country. They can relate to our pain. The fact that it wasn't all easy, that there were so many dark days, is exactly the thing that gives hope to hearers and credibility to our message today.

Jesus told Paul he wanted to use his past as a tool for people to receive forgiveness. Your story can be the vehicle God uses for others to find forgiveness from their sin and their past. God has uniquely allowed the events of your past to be such that others will find relevance in them. When they see someone with your story and your past walking in freedom and life today, God will use that to inspire them to seek forgiveness, healing, and freedom.

Jesus also told Paul he would leverage Paul's past so others could find a place among the family of God. And God wants to use your past to do the same thing. Think of it: when we surrender our dark past to Jesus, refuse to live under condemnation, and embrace our appointment, God will actually use us to help others find acceptance and a place in God's family.

OUR PAIN HAS CREATED SPACE FOR OTHERS

Some of the most humbling moments of my life occur when pastors or leaders approach my wife and me after they've heard us tell a portion of our story, and they communicate that they finally feel that they have people they can relate to. Each fall we host an event for pastors and wives at Next Level Church. The purpose is not so much about downloading information as it is about creating an environment where couples can feel that they belong.

On the final night of the weekend, we have a time of prayer over the couples and create space for God to speak to their hearts and receive ministry. Just before our time of prayer, I've said to all of the couples, "If in the past, your ministry experience with leaders has been less than great, or it has been painful, I want you to know that tonight can be a night when you receive a fresh start and a new covering. If you want or need to be connected to something different from where you've come from, consider yourself home."

Many couples have broken down and shared their stories of pain. They've talked of loneliness and fatherlessness. In those moments I can't help but think back to sitting on the bed of our two-bedroom apartment, thankful we didn't choose bitterness, but instead chose to allow God to take our dark and painful past and leverage it for others' good.

A QUICK PERSONAL THOUGHT

It's possible the stuff of your past has left a residue on your present that you just can't seem to clean off. In other words, if you've got junk you just can't seem to defeat, see a counselor; do whatever it takes. I saw a counselor for a long time to help me process through the unhealthiness I had seen and the pain we went through. It was the best decision I could have made. If your past is still haunting your present, take the time and make the investment to dig that stuff out! There's too much at stake not to do that. Your life is too short and your story is too important to let your past keep impeding your future. We need you, underdog, to take control of your past so you can begin to leverage it for others.

TheUnderdogsBook.com/ch2

**SCAN HERE FOR BONUS CONTENT ABOUT
"WHEN YOU FEEL LIKE QUITTING."**

3

UNDERDOG EXCUSE #3

"My Reputation Is Too Scarred"

(JACOB)

{ The man asked him, "What is your name?"
GENESIS 32:27 NIV }

ONE PROBLEM WITH MOVING ACROSS THE COUNTRY TO start a church is that you don't know anybody. Now, this is an issue not just for attendance but also when you're trying to assemble equipment for your new church on the cheap. Since we had only $9,200, every penny mattered. The good news was my buddy knew a guy in Pennsylvania who was a friend and could get us a good deal on the sound equipment we needed for Next Level Church.

A few weeks later, when the gear started arriving at my front door, it was all labeled "Next *Rebel* Church." The friend thought that would be funny. So for the next several weeks, every few days the postman walked boxes up to the front door and looked at us funny. I didn't think much of it at the time; I was just happy to see our stuff.

One day, though, the mail guy came to our door and said, "I just have to ask, is that really the name of your church?"

It caught me off guard at first, but then I looked down to see him pointing at the label "Next *Rebel* Church." When I smiled and said no, he laughed and said, "Okay, good, because I just kept thinking, *Man, these guys must be really angry at somebody to name their church Next* Rebel." We had a good laugh. And to this day, every once in a while, when talking about our church with my wife, I will refer to it as "Next Rebel Church."

Never underestimate the power of a label.

LABELS ARE POWERFUL THINGS

We live in a world fixated on labels. Our society is quick to label anyone and everyone. A politician is a *right-wing conservative*. A celebrity struggling with the paparazzi is *angry*. A thirty-five-year-old injured quarterback is *washed-up*. Labels are everywhere, including in the Bible. In the Old Testament, we find the story of a guy who was labeled. He was a man God desired to use in a great way, but he had been tagged from birth with a label he just couldn't seem to shake. His name was Jacob, and his label was an excuse keeping him from his destiny.

A LITTLE BACKSTORY

In the book of Genesis, we find the story of this labeled underdog named Jacob. He was the grandson of one of the great establishers of faith, Abraham. Abraham was the guy who believed God for a son in faith and consequently ended up being the father of God's nation, Israel. God put his hand on Abraham, then his son Isaac, and then Isaac's son, Jacob. This family tree became the nation of Israel, the people of God.

In Genesis 25, the Bible records that Jacob had a twin brother, Esau. But when the twins were coming out of the womb, Jacob was clinging to the foot of Esau. Quite literally from the day they were born, Jacob was always trying to one-up his brother. That moment and that story marked Jacob's life. In fact, his very name, *Jacob*, means "undercutter," "usurper," or "deceiver." At the very beginning of his life, he was given a label. Every time his mother told the story of the twins' birth, the label was reinforced. Jacob was a labeled underdog.

Throughout Jacob's childhood, it affected him. Growing up, Jacob saw himself as the tag that had been placed on him. He was just as he had been named to be: a liar, an undercutter, a deceiver.

At one point, he tricked his older twin brother, Esau, into giving him the birthright for the family, which was everything to a firstborn. Later he tricked his father, Isaac, into giving him the blessing of the family. At every turn, Jacob couldn't get past his label. No matter what he tried, he couldn't make the change necessary to get a different outcome in his life.

WHAT'S YOUR LABEL?

I love giving nicknames to people close to me. I like to think these fun little labels let people know they are special to me. And the nicknames I give people often evolve over time. For example, my sister-in-law has the same name as my wife, Sarah. So when I first met her more than a decade ago, I started calling her *H*, as in the last letter of her name. *H* became *Aich*, which became *Hitch*. *Hitch* became *Hitachi*, which then morphed into *Hitchy-getchi-gumba-now-you-gotta-rumba*. At the time of this writing, her current nickname is *Gumba*. But don't worry. It will probably change by Christmas.

Every one of us has been given some labels at different points in life. Most of them are placed on us by others. Some are deliberate. Others are inadvertent. Some are positive, but some are not. A misspoken word in a heated conversation. A name yelled in anger. A tag given to us from a frustrated parent. Just like Jacob. And for many of us, no matter how hard we try, we just can't seem to shake it.

Maybe you've played the other side. Ever labeled someone else? It might have been accidental or innocent, but I'm willing to bet each of us has been the giver of a label at some point. It's crazy to consider that God would give us such power over someone else's life, isn't it? To think that by the very words we speak, we can change someone's destiny forever. I'm sure Isaac had no idea of the power of his words in the delivery room that day when he named his second son Jacob.

A FEW LABELS OF MY OWN

Throughout my life I've had my fair share of labels. From the time I was in fifth grade, I've always been labeled *musical* and *theatrical*. Occasionally, some of my closest friends will label me *animated* and even *overdramatic*, which, if I'm being honest, I can be from time to time. I have definitely never been labeled *outdoorsy*, *woodsy*, or *earthy*, that's for sure.

When I travel and speak, I'm often labeled the *energy guy* or the *hyperguy*. What can I say? People tend to get more out of a teaching when they stay awake! On our church staff, I wear the label *strategic*. Everything we do as a church is well thought through and strategic.

One of the labels I'm most proud of happened at the bachelor party before my best friend Mike's wedding. We were hanging out playing paintball, and afterward, while we were eating pizza and wings, Mike took each one of his groomsmen aside and gave him a special thank-you gift for being in his life and in the wedding. When I opened my gift, it was a money clip with the word *Brave* engraved on it. The word caught me off guard because never in my life had anyone given me that label. And certainly when I think of myself, *brave* is one of the last ways I would describe myself. (See the "not outdoorsy" comment earlier.)

GOD OF THE UNDERDOGS

Before I could question his choice of words, Mike explained how the label came about. A year or so before, he and I had had some hard conversations where, as he says, I "put the friend above the friendship." Consequently, he went on to explain, he wouldn't be marrying the girl of his dreams the next day had I not been brave enough to have those conversations and do what was right for him, even if it cost me my friendship in the process. I'll never forget that night, and I'll never forget the label I was given.

The labels we wear shape who we become.

Never underestimate the power of a label.

Of course, the labels I've described above are positive and some are even humorous, but as you well know, not all labels are fun, positive, or good. Many are mean, negative, or demeaning, and some are downright evil. The labels we wear shape who we become. And eventually, who we become catches up with us. That's what was about to happen to Jacob.

FACE-TO-FACE WITH HIS LABEL

Jacob's relationship with his brother diminished to such a degree that it reached a breaking point. Jacob found himself at a life-or-death crossroads. He had once again undercut, usurped, and deceived his older brother, Esau, and now Esau was mad. And by mad, I mean Esau had assembled the fighting boys, and they were coming to take Jacob's life.

Where we pick up the story, Jacob was at his wit's end, knowing his brother was coming for him in the morning. So Jacob turned in the only direction he knew to turn at a moment like that: he turned to God. But as we're about to see, even in turning to God, Jacob couldn't seem to get past his scheming and conniving ways.

> Then Jacob prayed, "O God of my father Abraham, God of my father Isaac, LORD, you who said to me, 'Go back to your country and your relatives, and I will make you prosper,' I am unworthy of all the kindness and faithfulness you have shown your servant. I had only my staff when I crossed this Jordan, but now I have become two camps." (Gen. 32:9–10 NIV)

In other words, "God, let me remind you that there's a whole lot at stake here." He continued, "Save me, I pray, from the hand of my brother Esau, for I am afraid he will come and attack me, and also the mothers with their children" (Gen. 32:11 NIV).

Can you hear the manipulation in his voice? Even with his back against the wall, even in this sincere moment of prayer, Jacob couldn't get past himself. He was trying to deceive and manipulate God. For those of us who remember the TV show *Leave It to Beaver*, we could say Jacob was trying to Eddie Haskell God right here: "God, if not for me, save me because of the mommies and the babies!" Who did he think he was kidding? He was talking to the God of the universe, for crying out loud, and he was trying to manipulate him? His next comment was just as ugly: "You have said, 'I will surely make you prosper and will make your descendants like the sand of the sea, which cannot be counted'" (Gen. 32:12 NIV).

Jacob was doing his best to remind God of his promise to him and his family. But poor Jacob couldn't get past the label that had been firmly fixed on him since birth. He had been labeled a deceiver, and that's exactly who he was, even with God. What did Jacob decide to do next? "He spent the night there, and from what he had with him he selected a gift for his brother Esau" (Gen. 32:13 NIV).

So after Jacob lay down to go to sleep, he suddenly had an idea: bribery. *If I can't get God to listen to me, then I'll try and bribe my brother, Esau. I'll try and pay him off in advance.* Look at his gift: "two hundred female goats and twenty male goats, two hundred ewes and twenty rams, thirty female camels with their young, forty cows and ten bulls, and twenty female donkeys and ten male donkeys" (Gen. 32:14–15 NIV).

How about adding three French hens and a partridge in a pear tree? Jacob was doing the only thing he knew to do. He was once again living up to the label placed on him. He had become the liar, the cheater, and the deceiver he was labeled to be. Next Jacob arranged his gift to give him the best possible chance of winning over his brother: "He put them in the care of his servants, each herd by itself, and said to his servants, 'Go ahead of me, and keep some space between the herds'" (Gen. 32:16 NIV).

In other words, "Space yourselves out so it looks like a parade of livestock floating by my brother, Esau."

> He instructed the one in the lead: "When my brother Esau meets you and asks, 'Who do you belong to, and where are you going, and who owns all these animals in front of you?' then you are to say, 'They belong to your servant Jacob. They are a gift sent to my lord Esau, and he is coming behind us.'" (Gen. 32:17–18 NIV)

Not the one who had been clinging to your heel since birth; not the one who had repeatedly lied to you and undercut you and deceived you all your life; not that guy. No, they were from *your servant* Jacob! Pretty disgusting stuff, isn't it? Then, at the end of this parade, the grand marshal himself was coming to serve you. Jacob was a misguided and deceived underdog whose label was about to cost him everything.

In keeping with the plan, Jacob sent all of his possessions, family, and servants across to the other side of the stream. Before coming face-to-face with his brother in the morning, Jacob wanted to be alone with God.

At the end of all his scheming and deceiving, Jacob knew deep down what he needed most was God. Jacob knew his days of trying to change his label in his own strength were over. He knew if God didn't intervene, he was a dead man the next morning.

DEATH BY LABEL

It's quite possible you can identify completely with Jacob. You know what it is to have a label placed on you and to have it define you. And as much as you've tried, no matter how hard you've fought it or denied it, you just can't seem to shake it. In fact, you've been tempted to believe you're going to have to wear it like a tattoo for the rest of your life. Worse yet, you've even been tempted to believe it will be the death of you.

If that's you, you must grab hold of this next statement:

YOU ARE MORE THAN YOUR LABEL!

Because we serve a God who is bigger than any label that's been placed on you, there's hope for you. Even if there's truth to your label, as there was in Jacob's case, you must know we serve a God who is able to remove the labels that have fixed themselves to our lives. We serve a God who removes them from underdogs like you and me every day!

A LIFE-ALTERING ENCOUNTER

Having sent all of his earthly possessions to the other side of the stream, Jacob was left alone with his thoughts, his actions, and his labels. But even when he thought he was alone, he found himself in the presence of the one far greater than he ever imagined: "So Jacob was left alone, and a man wrestled with him till daybreak" (Gen. 32:24 NIV).

How was it possible for Jacob to be alone and yet wrestle with *someone*? Theologians tell us that this "man" Jacob wrestled with was not a human being. Jacob was indeed alone. The being he wrestled with was a pre-Jesus personification of God. God himself came down that night to rip the label off Jacob once and for all. The Bible tells us that Jacob wrestled with God all night long: "When the man [God] saw that he could not overpower him, he touched the socket of Jacob's hip so that his hip was wrenched as he wrestled with the man" (Gen. 32:25 NIV).

Jacob's hip went out of its socket, and he was in excruciating pain as he wrestled with God all night. "Then the man said, 'Let me go, for it is daybreak.' But Jacob replied, 'I will not let you go unless you bless me'" (Gen. 32:26 NIV).

Jacob was desperate for God to remove once and for all the label that had hung around his neck like a noose. He was so desperate that he held on to God and would not let go. Jacob understood that if God didn't remove the label, he was not going to make it past tomorrow.

ARE YOU WILLING TO WRESTLE?

I believe the power to remove the labels in our lives is available to us today as well. But we must answer several questions: Are we willing to wrestle with God? Are we willing to do the hard work of pressing in to him like we never have before? Are we willing to hold on to him so tightly that it actually forces his hand? Are we willing to surrender our lives to his truth and his Word? Are we willing to believe what he says about us more than what others have said about us?

> Are we willing to believe what he says about us more than what others have said about us?

Are we willing to fight that kind of fight? God wants to remove the label from our lives and replace it with a new one, but we must be willing to set everything else aside and get in the ring with him. God is asking you and me today, "Are you willing to wrestle? Are you finished with making excuses and walking in defeat and doubt and discouragement? Are you willing to lay down the security and comfort that live inside the labels of your past and take up the new label I have for you?"

Because Jacob was willing to lay everything else aside and

51

be alone with God, God met him there, and a wrestling match ensued. A wrestling match that lasted all night. But then as daybreak was dawning, and seeing that Jacob was determined for God to remove his label, God did an interesting thing: "The man asked him, 'What is your name?'" (Gen 32:27 NIV).

Now, I don't know about you, but this question seems quite out of place to me. If I'm going to spend an entire night wrestling with someone, I want to know who the person is beforehand. That just seems obvious to me. Why would God ask such a silly question? Did he bump his head during the wrestling match? Was he confused? Was he delirious from lack of sleep?

No, God was not confused, nor did he bump his head during the match. In order for Jacob to change the label that hung over his life, God knew Jacob first had to admit what the label was. God understood the power of confession. Until we are willing to admit who we are, we can never become who he wants us to be.

Until we are willing to admit who we are, we can never become who he wants us to be.

So, as they were wrestling and the sun was beginning to rise, God said to Jacob, "Before I can do anything about your label, you have to be willing to own who you are, at the core of your being. Otherwise I can't help you become anything else."

What about you? Have you ever been willing to say out loud the label that's been placed over your life? In order to change your label, you must first admit that you have one.

What's your label? Will you say it out loud? Right now, I challenge you to just say it out loud. (Of course, if you're sitting in a coffee shop or public place, you might want to go outside or at least use your inside voice.) There is freedom in being able to admit the label that has hung over your head your entire life.

MY SAY-IT-OUT-LOUD MOMENT

Several years ago I was doing some soul-wrestling of my own that included seeing a counselor. During one of our sessions, he encouraged me to do something that—at the time—I didn't understand. As I began sharing how angry I was about a certain set of circumstances in my life, he finally stopped me and encouraged me to "follow my anger."

Not knowing what he meant, I asked him to explain. He said that our present circumstances often mask the real reason for our heaviness of heart. In other words, we can't see past our present hurt, pain, and problems to actually identify the root cause of what we're really upset about. Over the next hour, he helped me dig four or five layers down past my present circumstances into the true core issue.

Before our time was up, I blurted out, "I'm angry because ..." and vocalized something that had taken place close to a decade earlier in my life. When I said it out loud, it was as if the blinders came off my eyes, the fog lifted, and I just sat there looking at him for more than a minute, now clear on what I was *really* upset about. It wasn't my present circumstances; it was something that had taken place years before involving someone who was no longer in my life. I had been carrying around the hurt from a label, and it had affected my present. In the following weeks, God changed the label over my heart, and I've never been the same.

JACOB'S DECLARATION

When faced with the question, "What is your name?" Jacob was forced to declare who he was. So with all of the rawness within him, Jacob shouted at God: "Jacob" (Gen: 32:27 NIV).

"My name is deceiver. Liar. You want to know who I am, God? I'm a manipulator! I am the one everyone labels the bad kid. I'm the one no one trusts. You want to know who I am, God, well, guess what? *That's who I am!*"

But then a powerful thing happened. After Jacob declared his label to God, God stepped in and changed his label: "Then the man said, 'Your name will no longer be Jacob, but Israel, because you have struggled with God and with humans and have overcome'" (Gen. 32:28 NIV).

"Jacob, from now on you'll no longer wear the label you've worn in the past; today I'm giving you a new label. You will be called Israel. You have struggled with God and with human beings and have not let it get the best of you. The label you once wore, you'll never wear again."

Don't miss what was happening. On the surface this can look like a simple name change, but something supernatural was taking place in this moment. God was changing Jacob at the deepest level. Who Jacob believed he was, was no longer true. He used to be labeled a deceiver, but from then on he would be known as an overcomer.

At that point, Jacob turned it back on God. After all, if we're exchanging names, you go next: "Jacob said, 'Please tell me your name.' But he replied, 'Why do you ask my name?' Then he blessed him there" (Gen. 32:29 NIV).

I love this exchange because it didn't go both ways. Just because God made Jacob say his name out loud didn't mean he was bound to say his name out loud. God basically said to Jacob, "Who's asking?" God didn't need Jacob to change his label. God's name has been the same forever! His label has never changed! He is the same yesterday, today, and forever. We can trust in that fact with all our hearts.

But then the Bible records that God "blessed him." The one thing Jacob had wanted all his life was the blessing of the father. The one thing he had spent decades of his life manipulating and usurping to have was the blessing. And it was only after God changed the label over his life that God knew Jacob, now Israel, was ready to be blessed.

God wants to bless your life more than you can imagine. But God knows that as long as you're living under the labels placed on you in your past, you will not be able to receive and use his blessing effectively. Only after you allow God to change your label can you fully experience the blessing and favor of God.

MY JACOB MOMENT

In the spring of 2008, I had my Jacob moment. I learned some things about the leaders who had influenced me in the early days of my leadership journey. Things that were ugly and hard to hear. It felt like a punch in the gut. These men had been early heroes to me in the ministry and in my life. They were instrumental in my call to ministry as a teenager and in my ability to hear the voice of God.

Upon hearing this new truth, I reached a crisis moment of desperation in my faith and in my leadership calling. During that time I reached out to a pastor friend who had gone through a similar struggle when one of the greatest influencers in his life—and a nationally known leader—had been exposed of sin and a secret life.

When I called my friend, I shared my story and then listened to his. After about twenty minutes, I asked him a huge question: "Can anyone do this? I mean, honestly, can any leader in ministry really go the distance in our world today? Can anyone be successful in ministry *and* stay faithfully and happily married for fifty years?" I remember telling him, "Listen, if you tell me no, that it really can't be done and that we're all going to blow it in the end, then with all due respect, I'm out. I will walk away now and go do something else. The last thing I want to do is get twenty years down the road of ministry and then cause severe damage to the name of Jesus Christ, inflict pain on my wife and kids, and blow up everything."

After a long pause on the phone, my friend said to me, "Matt, the answer is yes. It is actually possible to make it. To live with integrity and be successful and not blow the whole thing up in the end." Then he said something that has shaped me from that day on. He said, "This is your Jacob moment. This is the moment when you get alone and wrestle with God." He continued, "Because the reality is, you're good. You're real good. And you can flip a switch right now and shut off on the inside, and no one will know for a long time. You can grow a really big church and influence a lot of people for a long time but be faking it on the inside. Because you're that talented and gifted. And for a while no one will know."

His next statement rocked me to the core: "But *you'll* know. You'll know that inside you're just faking it and going through the motions. You'll know that you've become nothing more than a professional minister.

"So, Matt, this is your Jacob moment." Those words rang in my ears. "The moment when you send everything else ahead. All your talent, your ability, your charisma, your personality, everything, and you get alone with God and you wrestle until he breaks your hip.

"This is the moment when you'll go one way or the other. And if you choose to fake it, someday CNN will show up at your door, and it will all come to light. But if you choose to wrestle and let God change who you are at the core, God will break your hip, and you'll forever walk differently. This is your defining moment, Matt. Fake it or walk with a limp. The choice is yours."

Fake it or walk with a limp. I remember standing there looking out the window of my office in silence on the phone, knowing that he was right. I had a choice to make. The next thing out of my mouth was, "Well, I think that's all I had to talk to you about." We both laughed, and I thanked him.

When I hung up, I knew I had only one choice: wrestle.

I had to choose to let God change me at the core of my being. I had to choose to let God change my identity and let it be the catalyst to a new approach to everything I was and everything I did for the rest of my life. That was my Jacob moment. That day I found a new label, and I've never been the same.

ARE YOU READY FOR A NEW LABEL?

God wants to change who you are, not just what you do. God wants to change you at the deepest level—the belief level. It's possible you have thought a relationship with God was about making a decision, praying a prayer, doing good stuff, and getting good outcomes. But that is not all a relationship with God is about. It is about a change of identity. It's not just about doing better, trying harder, doing more, or serving more. It's about understanding who God says you are and allowing that to change you from the inside out.

What do you believe about yourself? Jacob believed he was a deceiver because he had been labeled that his entire life. What labels have been placed on you? Who have others said you are? Who have you said you are? The ugly one? The failure? The not quite good enough? The skinny one? The fat one? The dumb one? The screwup? The short one? The reckless one? The one incapable of change? The addicted one? The unlovable one? The unworthy one?

Some of us have been carrying around inside of us a label like Jacob bore for our entire lives. We have believed it in our hearts for far too long. God wants to remove that from your life once and for all. If you're going to experience a label change, you must understand it will require a supernatural work of God in your life.

For Jacob it took a life-or-death circumstance. But it doesn't have to. It takes a willingness on your part to wrestle with God. God is looking for you to take a step toward him and say, "Okay, God, I'm ready. Change me from the inside out. Not just my decisions and my outcomes. Change who I believe I am." Are you ready to do that? I hope you will not let another day go by without getting alone with God and allowing him to change the label that's been holding you back for too long.

When you allow God to change the label over your life, it affects not only you but also every other relationship in your life. It will affect your entire family tree. From that moment on, Jacob's family tree was different. In fact, to this day there remains the nation of Israel on the earth. The label of Jacob is long gone, and the world is different because one underdog was willing to wrestle with God. I guess there's just one question left to ask:

Are you willing to wrestle?

TheUnderdogsBook.com/ch3

SCAN HERE FOR BONUS CONTENT ABOUT THE "JACOB MOMENTS" OF LIFE.

4

UNDERDOG EXCUSE #4

"My Dream Is Too Radical"

(JOHN THE BAPTIST)

> He went into all the country around
> the Jordan, preaching a baptism of
> repentance for the forgiveness of sins.
> LUKE 3:3 NIV

IN 1952, A TRAVELING MINISTER BY THE NAME OF REV. Everett Swanson was on a successful preaching tour of South Korea. During his time in that country, his heart broke for the countless orphans lacking life's most basic necessities: food, shelter, medical care, and education. Upon returning to the United States, overcome by a desire to do something, Rev. Swanson began to ask God for a vision to somehow change the destiny of these most precious underdog orphans.

A short time later he had an idea for a sponsorship program that paired caring individuals in the United States with individual children in impoverished countries. He used local churches to distribute aid to meet their needs. This concept had never been carried out before. His dream was a radical one. It was unproven, untested, and unknown. Determined not to let that excuse hold him back, Rev. Swanson stepped out in faith and launched his plan.

Today, we know his ministry as Compassion International, a global ministry helping millions of children around the world each year through partner sponsorships like the one Rev. Swanson dreamed of more than sixty years ago. His idea was radical. He was an unorthodox underdog who stepped out and changed the world.

RADICAL DREAMER

When I think of people with radical dreams in the Bible, my mind immediately races to a guy in the New Testament who was actually a cousin of Jesus. John the Baptist was an underdog with a radical dream to see God move in a new way. Many of us reading this can probably relate to that dream.

Now here's the thing: on the surface, John the Baptist doesn't seem like an underdog. In many Christian circles, he's considered more of a celebrity, hero, and rock star. We don't have to read too far into the life and ministry of John the Baptist before we find a guy who is eating bugs and dressing weird. (Sounds like a rocker already, doesn't he?)

But when we dig deeper into his story, we find a guy who didn't have his whole life and ministry handed to him on a silver platter. We find John, the underdog. And as we're about to see, he was an underdog with a radical approach to the dream in his life.

In the fifteenth year of the reign of Tiberius Caesar—when Pontius Pilate was governor of Judea, Herod tetrarch of Galilee, his brother Philip tetrarch of Iturea and Traconitis, and Lysanias tetrarch of Abilene—during the high-priesthood of Annas and Caiaphas, the word of God came to John son of Zechariah in the wilderness. (Luke 3:1–2 NIV)

A LITTLE BACKGROUND ON JOHN

Now, before you skim over all the names of apparently really important people who lived some two thousand years ago, I want to draw your attention to a couple of things by way of introduction to where we're going in this chapter. First, the life of John the Baptist was perfectly situated at a time in history when God was setting the stage for the entrance of Jesus.

Did you see the names of guys like Pontius Pilate, Annas, and Caiaphas? These are names of people who will show up later in the Jesus story. John, the underdog, was to play a major role in the story that God was telling, just before Jesus showed up on the scene and changed everything. John, the unorthodox underdog, was a setup for Jesus' appearing. (More on the relevance of that later.)

Second, Luke records that "the word of God came to John." In other words, John was hearing from God! Again, don't hurry past this point. Here's why: when you consider how unorthodox John was in his tactics and approach to ministry, it will be tempting to write him off as a kook, a freak, or worse, a heretic.

But John was hearing from God! Even with an unorthodox approach to his dream, God set him up to be an underdog in a lot of ways. And we must not overlook that John heard from God. His message was airtight and completely directed by the Lord for his day and hour.

By way of introduction, John was a preacher's kid—another one of those points that can go unnoticed if we're not looking for it. John's dad was Zechariah, the priest. In other words, Zechariah worked in their version of a local church. John was raised in a pastor's home, with all the presumptions a PK (pastor's kid) has to endure.

From the youngest age, I'm sure John grew up hearing things like, "You'll walk in your father's footsteps one day," and "You're a chip off the old block," or the spiritual version, "The Lord's hand is on you just like it was on your father." John probably grew up with a lot of pressure from the religious community to fit into the mold of the day. So imagine what a black sheep he was when, instead of going with the status quo and serving God like his dad and the previous generation did, he felt compelled to live his dream differently.

John was a way-out-there underdog. He didn't match up to the expectations placed on him. And his vision didn't fit into the box of the established religious institution of the day: "He went into all the country around the Jordan, preaching a baptism of repentance for the forgiveness of sins" (Luke 3:3 NIV).

John didn't do ministry like it had always been done. No, the

Bible says he went into all the country around the Jordan. In other words, he went away from the city, away from the established church, and started something brand-new.

BREAKING THE MOLD

In a lot of ways I can relate to John, and I'm guessing on some level, you can too. God is placing dreams inside hearts today. Dreams that don't fit the mold of so much of what has existed up to this point in our world. God is breaking the molds for how we change the world. Underdogs everywhere are being called upon to reinvent the ways we make a difference in the world to come.

In his book *The Reinventors*, business author Jason Jennings makes the case that all businesses and enterprises in general must pursue radical and continuous change in order to stay relevant and viable in their industry long term. He concludes, "Anyone who thinks that they'll get a free pass and that they don't have to constantly reinvent their business has their head in the sand" ([New York: Penguin, 2012], 4.)

I recently gave a talk on the rise of the emerging generation in leadership in our world today to an organization in the northern United States. After my talk, a leader in his fifties approached me to ask a question. As he shook my hand, he asked, "If it is true that the young generation are rising up in unorthodox ways, as you say, why don't we see more of them in our world today?"

Sensing the sincerity in his voice, I answered him by saying, "They are. They just aren't emerging through the traditional channels of the business and governmental systems we have long used to identify them. Leaders like Mark Zuckerberg, founder of Facebook, and Tony Hsieh, founder of Zappos.com, have built billion-dollar companies. They just have done so outside the boundaries of the typical, traditional business model."

I continued, "The vast majority of great companies leading in our economy today are not those that have been around for a hundred years, but those founded in the last decade by twenty-something college students."

When it comes to the great ills threatening our world today, we are naïve to think they can be solved with yesterday's solutions. God is looking for a new breed of underdogs who will be willing to venture into the countryside like John and blaze a new trail. I believe you can be one of them.

BACK IN THE EARLY DAYS

In the early years of planting Next Level Church, we felt like total outsiders in the church world, but we were committed to the vision that God had placed in our hearts: to see him do a new thing in our generation. Years before, while Sarah and I were just teenagers dating in our youth group, we used to sit in the car after dates and talk about how we believed our generation would change the way the church did church. Not change the message. Change the methodology to reach a new generation. John the Baptist must have believed the same thing. He didn't let the excuse of his dream being too radical stop him, and we must not either. There is too much at stake.

John challenged an established religious system that had

been effective and in place for several generations. Who was he to think he had a different approach that would appeal to a new group of people? How arrogant to believe he could keep the message the same but change the method to achieve the same result of life change!

John was an unorthodox underdog.

NOW TO YOU

I hope right now you're thinking of that crazy dream you've had of doing something great for God. That dream to start a business with a different model than you've ever seen before or to start a humanitarian organization capable of meeting a need in our world in a way no one has. That idea to mobilize your neighborhood to make a difference in a needy family going through a hard time. Or that concept for a small group in your church that could connect to a group of people no one else is connecting to.

> The God of the universe is placing visions and dreams in our hearts that will change our world and reach lost people like never before.

If you have ever thought, *My dream is too out-there*, you are not alone! One of the most effective figures of the entire Bible was just as out-there, just as rogue, just as unorthodox in his vision from God as you are. And remember, he did hear from God! John the Baptist was a way-out-there underdog, just like you are today.

I believe we are standing as forerunners before a mighty appearing of Jesus like our world has never seen. The God of the universe is placing visions and dreams in our hearts that will change our world and reach lost people like never before.

He is releasing creative ideas that have never been imagined before to impact a lost, hurting, and broken world. God is raising up unorthodox underdogs who are poised to proclaim the same message of hope, freedom, and life in Jesus Christ in a new, albeit unorthodox way. And I believe you can be one of those underdogs.

It turns out that Scripture actually predicted the emerging of an unorthodox approach. In the next few verses of our story, Luke referred to an Old Testament passage in Isaiah that predicted John's and our approach:

> *A voice of one calling in the wilderness,*
> *"Prepare the way for the LORD,*
> * make straight paths for him.*
> *Every valley shall be filled in,*
> * every mountain and hill made low.*
> *The crooked roads shall become straight,*
> * the rough ways smooth.*
> *And all people will see God's salvation."*
> (LUKE 3:4–6, REFERRING TO ISA. 40:3–5 NIV)

Isaiah actually predicted "a voice" would come on the scene right before Jesus' arrival and would be unorthodox. The voice wouldn't use the same tactics as others before it. This voice would chart a new course with new, unorthodox methodologies capable of capturing the attention of our world like never before. John was that voice two millennia ago, and we are that voice today! God has placed a vision to change your world in your heart. And God is calling you to be a voice.

PRIORITIES OF JOHN'S APPROACH

If you have read this far into the book, I hope you're convinced of your underdog status, and you're convinced you are a candidate for God to use to change our world in some way. Good! But you're probably starting to wonder, *Okay, Matt, I get it. What do I do now? Where do I start? How do I proceed?*

Obviously, it's impossible for me to know what direction you will need to go or the sequence of steps you will need to take to pursue your dream and change your world. However, I do believe the first step is the same for all of us. And that step is to get the foundation to our approach right—at the heart level. To do that, we need to look no further than John. Five priorities laid the foundation for John's approach to pursuing his dream, and following his lead will set the stage for every step we take toward our dreams in the future. "John said to the crowds coming out to be baptized by him, 'You brood of vipers! Who warned you to flee from the coming wrath? Produce fruit in keeping with repentance'" (Luke 3:7–8 NIV).

Wow! Stop right there. Feel free to catch your breath for a second. John didn't wait to pull any punches with his audience. He got bold about his approach to his message real fast. Two sentences into John's message, and he was already tearing it up like a puppy with a newspaper! To be clear, John was not preaching some watered-down, tell-them-what-they-want-to-hear message. His introduction rang with phrases like "brood of vipers" and "coming wrath." Then he hit them with his first big priority.

CONSISTENCY

As John's ministry began to grow in popularity, people showed up and were being baptized, even though their hearts weren't in the right place. They saw baptism as the membership card of the cool club rather than as a testimony of true life change. Seeing a lot of people signing up but not living the life to back it up was not okay with John. His heart was for their lives to be consistent with the message they were professing by being baptized.

In other words, John was saying to his listeners, "Don't get in the pool and be baptized if you're not going to live it out in your daily life. If all you're interested in is a ceremonial deal or to be a member of some baptismal club, then don't bother. Your life must back up your mouth." John's approach to his message and his dream centered on *consistency*.

Never has consistency been more necessary in the lives of those who seek to change the world. We are living in an age when those of us who profess faith in Jesus Christ must back it up with more than just words. The world is screaming to the church today, "Show me consistency between what you say and what you do, or shut up already."

John's challenge to his listeners is our challenge as well. What about us? Are we living our lives in a consistent way? Or are we merely paying lip service to a cool program we want to be a part of? John's underdog message began with consistency.

CONSISTENCY, NOT PERFECTION

In the early days of our church, the going was pretty rough. Our equipment was old and beat-up, and we didn't have a lot of money. Things weren't flashy. And quite honestly, even what we did on the stage was not too pretty.

After one particularly rough Sunday at our movie theater church "home," I said to my wife, "I don't know why anybody comes back to this church. After today, I wouldn't even want to come back." Now, in this tender, vulnerable moment, one would expect my wife to say something like, "No, honey, that's not true. Today was really good. Your message was great, and it was better than you thought." However, that's not what she said.

Sarah made this pointed comment: "You know, we just have to remember that people come back to our church as much for what we're *not* as for what we are." Ouch! After the initial sting of her comment wore off, she explained what she meant. She wasn't being derogatory or condescending in what she said. Rather, she was saying that people aren't looking for perfection; they're looking for consistency and authenticity.

Seeking more than all the bells and whistles, prim and polish of a mature church, people who came to a movie theater church in those days were looking for consistency in the people they interacted with and from the leaders up front. Since those early days in the theater, that is exactly what we've always sought to be.

Consistency matters in the pursuit of our dream. It did for John. It did for us. And it matters to you.

CHECK YOUR MOTIVES

An additional piece of the equation when it comes to consistency is to do a motives check. Our motives matter. God has not called us to use our lives for our own glory and gain. He has called us to lay down our lives for his glory and other people's gain. The motives behind our dreams matter a lot. Consistency is only found long term when our motives are right.

When we place our lives against the backdrop of John's message, how do we line up? Why do we want to do what we want to do? What are our true motives? Is it for our own pleasure or gain? Or is it for the advancement of God's message on the earth? Do we truly care about people, or are we just in it to be a part of the club?

John's message placed a priority on consistency. He said,

> Do not begin to say to yourselves, "We have Abraham as our father." For I tell you that out of these stones God can raise up children for Abraham. The ax is already at the root of the trees, and every tree that does not produce good fruit will be cut down and thrown into the fire. (Luke 3:8–9 NIV)

John continued his message of consistency by reminding his listeners not to fall back on someone else's faith or consistency to carry them through. Either our faith is personal and authentic, or it is nothing. And the way to know the consistency of our faith is to examine the fruit of our lives.

When we look at the roots of our lives and see no fruit, John said the ax is already being swung. In other words, we cannot hope to live our dreams if what we see on the outside and who we are on the inside are not consistent.

GENEROSITY

After being challenged on their consistency, the crowd posed a question that led John to expound on the second priority of his approach to his dream.

> *"What should we do then?" the crowd asked. John answered, "Anyone who has two shirts should share with the one who has none, and anyone who has food should do the same." (Luke 3:10–11 NIV)*

The second priority of John's unorthodox message centered on *generosity*. He told his listeners that those who had excess ought to share it with someone else, be it food, clothes, or whatever. John's desire was to expose his audience to the essence of the heart of God, which is one of powerful generosity.

When it comes to the foundation for living our dreams, generosity must be at the very center. God uses generosity to demonstrate his love to our world in ways our words never can.

In fact, I believe generosity in the body of Christ could be one of the leading characteristics that will differentiate us from other religions of the world in the years to come.

For many other religions, the core of their message to their followers is narcissistic and self-focused: "If you serve the god we proclaim, it will end up making your life better." That is their primary message. The message of Christ, however, is completely the opposite.

Jesus boldly said, "Whoever wants to save their life will lose it, but whoever loses their life for me will find it" (Matt. 16:25 NIV). The message of Jesus is a selfless one. Generosity must be at the core of every underdog who follows Jesus and longs to make a difference in our world. It was a defining characteristic for John the Baptist, and it is a defining characteristic of the unorthodox thing God wants to do through you.

GENEROSITY IN REAL TIME

Sarah and I have always tried to live our lives with a generosity-first mind-set. In other words, we don't wait to see if there's any excess left over to be generous. We believe in giving God the first 10 percent of all our increase. We believe the tithe, as it is called in the Bible, is the starting point for generosity. As a parent, if I give one of my sons a bag with one hundred pieces of candy in it, is it too much for me to ask for him to give me ten pieces of candy back? That's the tithe. God has given us so much, and all he asks in return is for us to give him the first one out of every ten we receive. That has always seemed like a pretty good deal to us. We love giving the first of all our increase to God's local church. That's the beginning of generosity.

Additionally, we believe in the power of sowing seed above and beyond the 10 percent we give to the local church. When we have a need arise in our lives, we believe in giving a generous seed before we can see how God is going to come through and meet our need. I could tell you story after story of how God has come through for us time and time again when we have given in advance of a need. It's the principle of sowing and reaping. Not that God is a giant slot machine, but He is a loving, heavenly Father who responds to our faith.

And yes, there's always that little knot in our stomach when we're writing that check, but it is quickly erased with the greatest sense of peace and joy knowing that God is taking care of us. We love watching God show up in miraculous ways every time!

Generosity will look different for each of us, but one thing is sure: as you pursue your dream, God will call you to lead with generosity. That is how your message will look different to the world. What step of generosity could you take today to put your faith in action for your dream? Maybe it is taking the step to begin tithing. Maybe it is writing a check to someone else who's doing what you want to do. Maybe it is volunteering to help someone else's dream come true. How you use the talents, resources, and finances God has given you affects how your dream comes to pass. Live generously, and watch what God will do.

INTEGRITY

"Even tax collectors came to be baptized. 'Teacher,' they asked, 'what should we do?' 'Don't collect any more than you are required to,' he told them" (Luke 3:12–13 NIV).

The third priority of John's approach to his dream was *integrity*. When men who were notoriously known in their society as crooks heard the message, they asked what they were supposed to do. John's reply was, "Do what's right! Don't steal from people and cheat people. Just be honest and treat other people the way you would want to be treated."

God desires a return to integrity among the underdogs he chooses to use today. And yet, never has temptation been so prevalent and easily accessible. If we're going to have credibility as we live our dreams, we must hold ourselves to a higher standard where integrity is concerned.

We must not allow ourselves to be disqualified by sin. Because temptation is so glaring and constant in our world today, we need an increase in true accountability and openness with one another. As underdogs, we must commit to not trying to do life alone. Rather, we must embrace the idea of doing life together and confessing sin with other believers whom we allow to be close to us. James 5:16 gives us the most simple and potent prescription for overcoming temptation: "Confess your sins to each other and pray for each other so that you may be healed" (NIV). This is the path to true healing in our lives. Confession and a commitment to pray for each other.

We need each other. Gone are the days of trying to overcome temptation in our lives alone. God never intended us to fight this battle alone. Is it possible God allows temptation to be so strong that we can't fight it alone? We must have others in our lives who are fighting with us if we are going to live the lives of integrity that God wants us to live.

After all, if we were strong enough and capable enough to overcome the temptations we face by ourselves, we would be tempted to think "more highly [of ourselves than we] ought to think," as Paul wrote (Rom. 12:3 NKJV). This thinking would lead us into even greater sin and temptation. You and I can't win the battle of temptation without others. God has set up our faith journeys so we need not only him but also his body in order to be strong and live out our faith well. Only when we lean on others in our weaknesses can we understand the meaning of true integrity.

ACCOUNTABILITY IN REAL TIME

A few years ago a couple of my close friends and I became frustrated by the lack of conversation in the church world around this topic of temptation. In our search for wholeness and accountability, that frustration led us on a journey toward depth and realness like none of us had ever seen. Was it awkward at times? Yes. Was it difficult to bring everything out of the dark and into the light? No question. But here's the resolution we reached:

> WHATEVER STAYS IN THE DARK GROWS IN ITS
> POWER OVER YOU, BUT WHATEVER IS BROUGHT
> INTO THE LIGHT LESSENS ITS POWER OVER YOU.

For the first time in all of our lives, we felt that we were actually living in true accountability and authenticity about the present condition of our souls. I have become convinced that until we get to that place of depth with one or two other people who know all of the dark and hidden places of our hearts, we'll never be able to live and function in the wholeness that God desires.

I don't know what that will look like for you or where you need to start. However, if you want to live your dream, integrity isn't an optional add-on to your life. It is the foundation of what you are doing. Take the first step with a close friend. Dare to go deeper, open up, share your story, and then get consistent in a regular time to connect and ask each other the tough questions. Then and only then can you understand true integrity.

CONTENTMENT

Then some soldiers asked him, "And what should we do?" He replied, "Don't extort money and don't accuse people falsely—be content with your pay." (Luke 3:14 NIV)

The fourth priority of John's approach to his dream was *contentment*. When soldiers asked him how they should respond to his message, his reply centered on their not taking advantage of people and their being content with their pay. Talk about practical.

Once again, John's message rings true for us today. Contentment in our hearts toward things will lay a foundation for what God is able to do through us in the future. My friend Mike openly shares how he and his wife willingly drive an older, higher-mileage car so they can live more generously and be better stewards. They crossed a line in their hearts of knowing the difference between what they want and what they need. The contentment they have found has opened the door to huge blessing in their lives.

Contentment is the key to true freedom. When we learn to be content with what we have and abandon the race for more, bigger, better, and newer, we begin to experience freedom very few people know or understand.

I COULD; I JUST CHOOSE NOT TO

One of the greatest statements of freedom I've ever heard is: "I could; I just choose not to." When we reach this place in an area of our lives, that's when we're truly living free. For example, when we can say, "I could drive that kind of car; I just choose not to," we're free. Or, "I could live there; I just choose not to." Or, "I could wear that, do that, go there, drink that; I just choose not to." That's when we know we're content and free.

That's true freedom, isn't it? In his book *We Are All Weird*, author and marketing expert Seth Godin defines true freedom as "the ability to choose." Contentment in our lives is the doorway to experiencing true freedom.

So what about you? What could living at a level of greater contentment look like for you? What sacrifice could you make today that could have a direct impact on someone else's tomorrow? Who knows? You just might find a new level of freedom on the other side of that decision.

POINTING TO JESUS

The people were waiting expectantly and were all wondering in their hearts if John might possibly be the Messiah. John answered them all, "I baptize you with water. But one who is more powerful than I will come." (Luke 3:15–16 NIV)

The final priority of John's approach to his dream was his unrelenting desire to *point attention away from himself and toward Jesus.* John's life pointed others to Jesus. John boldly let all his listeners know he wasn't their answer. He was a messenger to point them to the one who was their answer: Jesus.

We must never lose sight of the fact that none of our hopes, dreams, visions, or ideas is about us. We, the unorthodox underdogs, are merely messengers sent by God to point the way for people to truly experience Jesus. After all, he alone is the one they need.

If we can remember that, we will have a strong foundation from which to pursue our dream. John the Baptist was a way-out-there underdog who pointed people not to himself and his radical dream but to Jesus, the ultimate underdog who could change their lives forever.

WHAT ABOUT YOU?

Who is your life pointing people toward? You or Jesus? When people interact with you or watch your life, who do they see? You or Jesus? God has not entrusted us with way-out-there dreams and ideas for our glory, fame, or recognition. He has given them to us for his glory, his fame, and his recognition. In 1952, Rev. Everett Swanson could have let his trip to South Korea be about his preaching ministry, his fame, and his success. Instead, he chose to use his life for a far greater goal: the benefit of the children of the world and the fame of Jesus.

May it be said of each of us that all we do points to one name alone: Jesus.

bit.ly/UnderdogsBook4

SCAN HERE TO LEARN MORE ABOUT THE MINISTRY OF COMPASSION INTERNATIONAL AND TO SPONSOR A CHILD.

UNDERDOG EXCUSE #5

"Nobody Recognizes My Potential"
(JESUS)

> When his parents saw him, they were
> astonished. His mother said to him, "Son,
> why have you treated us like this?"
> LUKE 2:48 NIV

SINCE I WAS EIGHTEEN YEARS OLD, I HAVE KNOWN I HAVE three callings in my life. The first is to pastor, which I have had the privilege of doing since we started Next Level Church in 2002.

The second calling is to write. I've always been in love with the practice of writing, and over the years it has played a minor role in my life. Avenues like my blog, MattKellerOnline.com, and an occasional magazine article or guest article for a website have served as the beginnings of that calling for me.

The third calling is to lead and influence other leaders at a high level. As you've heard previously in the book, before we moved to southwest Florida to start Next Level Church, God had given us a small measure of national influence with the little fellowship of churches we were a part of in the Midwest. So when we moved to Florida in 2002, it was a difficult transition for me to go from being a medium-sized fish in a small pond to being completely unknown in our city. We felt like we had fallen off the face of the earth.

My wife, Sarah, actually made the comment a few weeks after moving of how weird it was to walk through Walmart and think, *Nobody knows me here. No one in this store knows who we are right now.* We had moved to this area to do something great for God, and yet exactly zero people out of the half million in our county had any clue who we were. We had huge potential, but nobody could see it. We were underdogs with unseen potential.

For thirty of Jesus' thirty-three years on earth, he had limitless potential to heal, teach, and change the world, and yet it was completely unseen to *everyone* around him. Even his parents didn't see it!

UNSEEN POTENTIAL

In Luke 2, we find a story about twelve-year-old Jesus that illustrates this perfectly. His entire family had taken a road trip to Jerusalem, and on their way home, because they were traveling en masse, nobody apparently noticed preteen Jesus' absence.

After a few days of traveling, Jesus' earthly parents, Mary and Joseph, got word that nobody seemed to have seen Jesus in, well, a few days. After what I am sure was some intense investigating, they realized he was not with them at all. They had left the Son of God behind on a road trip! (I lost one of my boys for like eighteen seconds at Target one time, and I felt like a total loser for weeks. Imagine losing the Son of God for a few days! Ouch.)

So Mary and Joseph made the three-day journey back to Jerusalem to find him. When they finally found him, he was in, of all places, the temple. Talk about adding to the guilt! Not only did they lose him, but when they finally found him, he was at church. Read what happened next: "After three days they found him in the temple courts, sitting among the teachers, listening to them and asking them questions. Everyone who heard him was amazed at his understanding and his answers" (Luke 2:46–47 NIV).

There was preteen Jesus doing the thing he was born to do. He was beginning to live his potential, and others were actually noticing. However, his parents' response was not so acknowledging: "When his parents saw him, they were astonished. His mother said to him, 'Son, why have you treated us like this?'" (Luke 2:48 NIV).

Did you get that? His parents were astonished, but not in a good way. They weren't astonished in the same way the religious guys had been. They were astonished by what they percieved as his thoughtlessness and carelessness toward them. Rather than see his potential, they chose to focus on themselves. *Jesus, how could you do this to us?*

Imagine being Jesus in this moment. He must have been

thinking, *Are you kidding me? You can't be serious, Mom and Dad. Do you not remember who I am? Did you forget the whole virgin birth thing and the angel showing up? Seriously, I'm the Son of God bursting with potential, and all you can focus on is how much inconvenience I've caused you?*

If this were happening in our day, preteen Jesus surely would have added, "Whatever!" Then he would have grabbed his smartphone and stormed off in disgust to post a rude Facebook comment about his mom and dad. Of course, he didn't do that. But he did actually say to his earthly parents, "Didn't you know . . . ?" (Luke 2:49 NIV).

Jesus must have felt that his potential was going unseen and unnoticed. Jesus knew what he was capable of and what he would one day accomplish, and yet the world around him couldn't see it yet!

EVER FELT LIKE THAT?

Maybe you've felt that way in your life. I'm quite certain every person reading this right now has felt that way at some point. Perhaps your parents can't seem to see what you see for your life. Maybe a teacher or a coach always seems to overlook your potential and call on someone else. Maybe a boss or a leader who, no matter how much effort you put in or how high your numbers are, never seems to give you the credit you deserve.

Every one of us, like Jesus, has had those moments when we've sat on the sideline thinking, *I have potential. I have thoughts. I swear my ideas are valid! I know I could do this if they would simply give me a chance. Pass me the ball. I will take the shot. I can make it. Trust me!*

And to make matters worse, some of us have seen opportunities go by, and no one ended up doing anything about it. Nobody got picked, and our company, our team, or our family ended up paying a big price because whoever had the power to choose ended up choosing no one rather than choosing us.

SOMETHING TO SAY AND NOBODY TO LISTEN

About four years into our church plant, things started to take off. We were gaining traction and momentum. We had grown from four people in a coffee shop to more than three hundred in two services in our rented movie theater. Along the way, we had begun to learn some lessons on how to grow a church, how to develop leaders, and so forth. During that season I actually wrote a book, *The Up the Middle Church*. The book was a collection of many of those lessons and reproducible principles we had learned in the early years of starting our church.

We believed we had something to say but quickly discovered not too many people wanted to listen. It was a frustrating season for me personally, especially in light of two callings I felt were on my life: to write and to influence other leaders. I could see the potential of our voice, but it was going unheard by others.

When I finished the manuscript for *The Up the Middle Church*, I presented it to several Christian publishers. About a half dozen actually took the time to read it and have a conversation with me. However, I quickly learned that getting a publisher to talk to you is all about who you know. But getting a publisher to give you a book contract is all about who knows you.

Over the course of a year I heard the same message again and again: "Your principles are solid and you are a good writer, but not enough people know who you are." I tried to explain to them this would add to the credibility of the book. After all, the book was about being an "Up the Middle Church," not a long-bomb, big church everyone knew. They didn't buy that. I felt like an underdog with unseen potential.

(Today, much is being written about the need to build a platform by leaders like Michael Hyatt, Seth Godin, Jeff Goins, and others. I highly recommend Michael Hyatt's book *Platform: Get Noticed in a Noisy World.* This is a must-read for anyone desiring to create a presence and make an impact on the world. Back then, however, information like that was less readily available.)

Being an underdog with unseen potential can feel discouraging, disheartening, and demotivating. Many dreams go unfulfilled because of this underdog excuse. I'm sure you've felt the sting of an experience like that. I have, and so did Jesus.

BACK TO JESUS

When you study the life and ministry of Jesus, you discover this incident when he was twelve years old was not the last time his potential was overlooked. Even after his public ministry began, there were still many doubters and skeptics.

For example, his siblings and family didn't realize his potential. In Matthew 12:46, Jesus was teaching a large group of people, and his family rolled up and was like, "Hey, Jesus, stop everything! We want to talk to you." Can you imagine what Jesus must have felt in that moment? *Seriously, you guys? Come on. Can't you see I'm kind of busy here communicating the words of eternal life!*

But they couldn't see it. They couldn't clearly see Jesus' potential even after he started preaching and teaching and affecting people's lives. Perhaps like Jesus, you have family or peers who can't seem to see your potential. In our lives there will be those who cannot see our potential. As much as we long for their affirmation or even just their acknowledgment, somehow they don't seem able to give it.

Another group of people who wouldn't see Jesus' potential were the Pharisees. They were constantly discrediting and questioning his teachings, his miracles, his authority, and his ministry. There must have been times when Jesus wanted to go all Jedi Force on them like Yoda and throw them across the room.

The Pharisees represented those with the perceived control and power in his world. In our lives there are those with power who won't see our potential either. Maybe it's the boss or the professor. Maybe a team captain or a coach. All of us have people in our lives whom we feel have the power to change our destiny, but for some reason, unknown to us, they don't.

Pilate was another leader in Jesus' life who refused to see his potential. He let peer pressure from the crowd sway his decision to recognize Jesus' potential. In fact, when Jesus was standing before him, Pilate actually got a little lippy with Jesus. He asked him, "Don't you realize I have power either to free you or to crucify you?" (John 19:10 NIV).

Pilate was basically saying, "Jesus, I have the power to recognize your potential if you'll say and do the right things right now." And in that moment, Jesus boldly replied, "You would have no power over me if it were not given to you from above" (John 19:11 NIV).

Jesus understood something about unrecognized potential. God's role and God's timing mean everything. Pilate represented those who knew better but refused to get past outside pressures to validate it. In our lives there will be those who refuse to see our potential too. No matter how much data they have or proof they can see, they just will not allow themselves to be associated with us.

The crowds around Jesus during his ministry on earth wanted to see his potential. They knew something was there, but it was still not entirely revealed. Many believed and were in awe, but not even they had a complete enough picture to validate it. One minute they were shouting and praising Jesus, and a few days later they were crucifying him. Jesus was an underdog with unseen potential just like you and me.

THE DANGER OF OUR UNSEEN POTENTIAL

The greatest danger connected to this underdog excuse is to let those who don't see our potential keep us from reaching it. Let me say that again because you've got to get it:

WE MUST NOT LET THOSE WHO DON'T SEE OUR
POTENTIAL KEEP US FROM REACHING IT!

A season of unseen potential can cause us to think thoughts like, *Why bother?* and *Why even try?* Speaking personally, I have been in that place many times. In my youth ministry days, I felt it. When I was traveling nationally, I felt it. Since we planted

> The greatest danger connected to this underdog excuse is to let those who don't see our potential keep us from reaching it.

our church, I have felt it countless times. This is a great danger to every underdog. If you are in one of those seasons, don't give up! God sees your potential. He is for you and with you and believes in you more than you even know.

UNTIL PHARAOH CALLS

As I mentioned earlier in the book, the first several years of our church were some of the most difficult years of my life. This issue of unseen potential was one of the major reasons why. During those years, Mike Ash and I often referenced the Old Testament story of Joseph in the book of Genesis. (Joseph's entire story is in Genesis 35–50.)

Joseph was a biblical underdog with crazy potential to lead and influence his family, his nation, and the world; and yet those around him couldn't see it. He experienced some of the most horrific events imaginable and ultimately landed unjustly in prison for several years. Joseph, with all his unseen potential, was left to die in a cold, dark, lonely dungeon.

Joseph spent several years in confinement with no one but a baker and a butler to talk to. During that time he interpreted their two dreams, but other than that, he was helpless, lonely, and useless—except for the fact that God was not finished with him. After years of confinement and through a crazy set of circumstances that included the butler telling Pharaoh of Joseph's gift to interpret dreams, Joseph was finally summoned before the king.

Long story short, Joseph used his gift in the palace to interpret the dream of the king and found himself named second in command of the entire nation. He was able to lead not only his nation but also that entire region of the world through the worst famine they had ever seen. Joseph was an underdog who became a hero, but his journey included a dungeon season. Every hero's journey seems to include a dungeon season. Mine did.

I remember one particularly dark season a few years into our church plant. I was talking to Mike about how much more I felt we had to offer and how nobody seemed to recognize it. I was moping and complaining about it, but then Mike said something I have never forgotten.

He looked directly at me and said, "Yeah, man, I know. I can see it too. I can see what God will do through you. I can see your potential but . . ." And then what he said next changed me forever. He said, "I can see what God wants to do, but until Pharaoh calls, you're going to have to just go back to the dungeon and be faithful with your gift there. Find the butlers and the bakers, and use your gift on them."

Until Pharaoh calls . . .

Those three words changed my life. I could see my potential, and my wife and those close to me could see it; but until God ordered the steps of others who had the power to amplify our voice and call it up to a higher level of influence, no amount of kicking, screaming, crying, or whining on my part was going to change my situation.

YOUR UNSEEN POTENTIAL

If you believe the thing holding you back from your dream and your destiny is that no one will recognize your potential, you must know a few important things.

First, you need to know you're not alone. Everyone with a dream has felt that way at one time or another. Jesus felt that way. Joseph felt that way. I have felt that way. Take comfort on this journey of pursuing your dream in knowing the season you're in is completely normal and necessary.

> Everyone with a dream has felt that way at one time or another.

Second, you need to know this season is not a bad one. Human nature always causes us to run from pain. However, when we do, we forfeit the benefits a season of struggle and pain can bring.

Third, you must not let this season paralyze you. This is a big one for us underdogs. We are living in an instant-gratification-right-now-customizable reality. We live in a world where we can download music, books, and media instantly, find any information on Google in a matter of seconds, and know what's happening in our friends' lives in a few moments through Facebook, Twitter, and other social media.

Therefore, when it takes longer than a few days or weeks for a dream in our hearts to come to pass, the temptation is for us to get discouraged. It may take a few seconds to download a song, but

The lessons in the dungeon season prepare us for the palace.

when it comes to our dreams becoming a reality, we are still living in a world where it takes years for them to happen. Don't let it discourage you! Don't give up on your dreams! They will happen. God has you in this place for a reason. If you give up, get discouraged, or lose heart, you will forfeit the learning uniquely available to you right now.

The lessons in the dungeon season prepare us for the palace. Joseph wasn't ready. If God had given him the influence his potential made him capable of, he would have destroyed his family and his destiny. He thought he was ready, but God knew better.

Looking back, I can see that what I thought I was ready for, I actually wasn't ready for. I thought I was ready for a national voice and large-scale influence in my twenties, but I wasn't. God had a lot of rough edges he had to work off me, and the best place to do that was in invisibility. The psalmist told God, "My times are in your hands" (Ps. 31:15 NIV). I believe that now.

IN A SEASON OF "BETWEEN"

The obvious question then becomes, what do we do in the season between the conception of our dream and when it comes to pass? What are the priorities for the season between our potential and when Pharaoh calls? We must institute three key priorities in a season of "between" in our lives.

The first priority is that we must practice our gifts. The Bible records that Joseph interpreted the dreams of the butler and the baker while he was in the dungeon. I can guarantee you that Joseph could have practiced his vision gift on others who passed through the dungeon in his years down there. In the same way, we find preteen Jesus in the temple asking questions and even teaching during his season of waiting.

When I found myself in the season between my potential and Pharaoh calling, I found a unique way to practice my leading-other-leaders gift. At each leadership conference I attended, I tried to find two pastors who looked lonely and discouraged. After talking with them awhile, I got their cell phone numbers and promised to call them the next month.

A few weeks later a reminder popped up on my phone to "Call 2 Pastors," and I looked at my list and started calling guys. When they answered, I reminded them who I was (this only got awkward a couple of times), and then I asked them how it was going. Once they got past "Everything's great. My life is perfect," they eventually opened up and shared something that wasn't going so well. At that point, I shared a time when we experienced something similar and what we learned through the process. The help I offered added enough value to them that they started calling me. Over time, our tribe was born.

Today a few hundred pastors all over the country receive encouragement, strength, and ideas from me and others in our tribe. If I had waited for some big conference to call me so I could start using my gift to influence other leaders, I'd still be waiting! In my season between my potential and Pharaoh calling, I practiced my gift.

My advice to you is the same. Go find a baker and a butler, and start using your gift. Think small. You never know; they just might be connected to a pharaoh someday.

The second priority for the season between our potential and Pharaoh calling is to be faithful where we are. If we're not careful, we can focus our eyes so far ahead that we miss where we are. Something powerful happens in our hearts when we sow into another man's field. The principle of sowing and reaping is a powerful one laced throughout Scripture. Your present season is a test from the Lord. He wants to see if you will be faithful to grow where you're planted.

We cannot underestimate the testing of our hearts by the Lord to see if we will be faithful with someone else's dream before God opens the door for us to step into our dreams. If we are not faithful with little, how can we be trusted with much? Looking back on my story, I can see that much of my early days in ministry were about the Lord testing my heart. Would I be faithful to sow into another man's field? Could I be trusted with my own dream if I was not willing to build someone else's dream?

The further I go in my underdog journey, the more I am convinced this test never goes away. Even as a guy who is living his dream on many fronts today, I am still challenged often to give my time, talents, expertise, and resources to fields where I will never be able to reap a harvest.

The third priority of a "between" season is to learn everything we possibly can. As I mentioned in chapter 2, in the early years of our church, we decided we could learn something from everybody—good, bad, or otherwise. And that's what we did. There was never an article or a book we read, a church or business we visited that we were not looking, learning, and translating what we saw into our context.

To this day, we love visiting big churches around the country to learn, glean, and catch how and why they're doing ministry the way they are. We aren't intimidated or jealous. We want to be sponges to soak up as much learning as we possibly can when we have the opportunity.

Don't waste this season of waiting in your life. Commit to learning all you can during this season of "between."

MY PHARAOH-CALLING SEASON

My Pharaoh-calling season happened in the period of about a year. In April 2011, we moved our church into our first permanent location and within nine months grew from almost one thousand regular attendees to more than two thousand people. We were actually listed as the ninth fastest growing church in America in 2012 by *Outreach* magazine. That recognition opened the door to increased exposure and opportunity to share what we were learning with others. That was a Pharaoh call.

In the same year, the concept of coaching took off in the church world. Because we had been doing coaching for more than five years and had built the systems, curricula, and technology, we suddenly were seen as a thought leader in this arena. In a matter of a few months, some of the largest and most influential churches in America began calling to learn from us about how we were doing it. More Pharaoh calls.

In February 2012, ARC (the Association of Related Churches, the network of churches with which we have been affiliated for years) asked me to join their lead team. Another Pharaoh call.

Then in April 2012, the culmination of the three callings in my life came when a literary agent contacted me and helped make my dream of writing a reality. The book you now hold in your hands is the very proof that when God says it's time for Pharaoh to call, nothing can stop it! Just because the world around you can't, won't, or doesn't see your potential yet doesn't mean God is failing to work behind the scenes.

Take heart, underdog. Soon enough you will hear the sound of a phone ringing in the distance. Soon enough you will hear footsteps coming down the hall. Soon enough you will hear the rattling of keys outside your perceived prison door, and in that moment, you will see the blinding light of day streaming into the dark cell you feel you've been living in. And in that moment, you will hear a voice say, "Get cleaned up. Pharaoh wants to see you now."

Nobody saw Jesus' potential, and it led him to a bloody cross and a cold, dark grave. But after a season—three days, to be exact—God rolled back the stone, light invaded darkness, and for all of eternity *everyone will see his potential*!

TheUnderdogsBook.com/ch5

SCAN HERE FOR BONUS CONTENT ABOUT "WHEN PHARAOH CALLS."

6

UNDERDOG EXCUSE #6

"I'm Not Connected to the Right People"
(MEPHIBOSHETH)

{ Mephibosheth ate at David's table
like one of the king's sons.
2 SAMUEL 9:11 NIV }

THROUGH THE YEARS, THERE HAVE BEEN TIMES WHEN I wished my story wasn't my story. Times when I would hear of other pastors who took over a church and had several hundred people and a big budget from day one. Or times when I would hear of church planters who were connected to organizations or denominations that gave them tons of money to help them start their churches, while I was working in the back of a jewelry store to make ends meet.

If I'm being honest, there have been days along the way when I let the excuse of not being connected to the right people hinder me. Many underdogs fall victim to this very common excuse in the pursuit of their dreams. But as we will see in this chapter, feeling that we're not connected to the right people doesn't mean we're forgotten.

Where we come from, to whom we were born, and the connections we have are in the hands of the Lord. God knows who we are and the connections we need; our job is to trust him. He has been working our entire lives to position us where he wants us now and in the future.

The underdog of this chapter wasn't connected to the right people, but God still orchestrated his journey to position him right where he needed to be. To understand how he got there, we have to rewind a couple of decades to the story of his father, his father's friend, and an insecure dad.

HARD TO LOVE

At some point in our lives, we have known someone who was hard to love. A boss. A coach. A lady who cut in front of us this morning at the checkout line. A coworker. An in-law. In this chapter, we find an underdog we've met before, David, but this chapter is not about him directly. This chapter is about someone David knew. Let me set the stage.

EVERYTHING CHANGES WHEN
YOU KILL A GIANT

You'll remember from chapter 1 that David was anointed to be king, but he didn't live happily ever after. No, David was faced with a relational struggle that would affect him for the next twenty years of his life. This struggle tested David in ways he never imagined.

We learned in chapter 1 that David was chosen by God to become the next king over Israel (1 Sam. 16). Then David slew the great tormentor of their nation, Goliath (1 Sam. 17). It was a battle of epic proportions. A battle fit for a king. Except the king didn't fight it. Cowardly Saul hid in his tent while young David defeated the giant of their day. And this is where the story gets interesting.

After David killed Goliath and the army of Israel won the battle, King Saul came out of his tent and wanted to know about this David kid. Who was he? Where did he come from? What family was he from? After a few explanations were given, the king invited David to come back to the palace with him instead of going home to the sheep: "After David had finished talking with Saul, Jonathan became one in spirit with David, and he loved him as himself. From that day Saul kept David with him and did not let him return home to his family" (1 Sam. 18:1–2 NIV).

Shortly after arriving in the palace, David started hanging around with the king's son Jonathan. The two young men become instant friends, and a tight bond formed between them. A bond that took on covenant status: "Jonathan made a covenant with David because he loved him as himself. Jonathan took off the robe he was wearing and gave it to David, along with his tunic, and even his sword, his bow and his belt" (1 Sam. 18:3–4 NIV).

A COVENANT?

In our culture today, the idea of a covenant has been largely lost. Today, everything revolves around contracts. When you rent an apartment or get a loan from the bank, you sign a legally binding document called a contract. This document holds you responsible to make good on your end of the bargain. When we don't trust someone, we form a contract.

A covenant is completely different and much more powerful than a contract. A covenant is based *on* trust. Not just trust in the other person but trust in a God who is at work in the midst of the two people and has the power to hold them accountable.

The premise of covenant goes back to the days of Abraham. God made a covenant between him and Abraham concerning how God would bless Abraham's family and use him to impact all the nations of the world. Here we are centuries later still reaping the effects of the Abrahamic covenant. Covenants are powerful things.

BACK TO DAVID AND JONATHAN

In the covenant between David and Jonathan, the bond was so deep that Jonathan, the oldest son of Saul, the rightful heir to the throne, gave David his sword, his bow, and his belt. That was his way of letting the entire kingdom know David was like another son of the king, not just a son-in-law. (Saul's daughter Michal married David.) By giving David his sword, his bow, and his belt, Jonathan was letting the world know this brotherhood was a forever thing.

Let me paint the picture for you of David's life. He was young, good-looking, and famous. He was best friends with Jonathan and married to the king's daughter. Life should have been looking up, right? Unfortunately, King Saul didn't think as highly of David as most people did. Let's just say when you're used to getting all the attention and then along comes a young hotshot like David, things can turn ugly pretty fast. "Saul was afraid of David" (1 Sam. 18:12 NIV).

AIN'T NO PROBLEM LIKE AN IN-LAW PROBLEM

Now, to say David's father-in-law was hard to love is an understatement. King Saul was not just a little hard to live with; he was, in many regards, downright crazy! To make matters worse, he wasn't doing a very good job as king either, remember? It didn't take Saul long to realize God was with David but had departed from him. The more Saul thought about it, the more freaked out he became: "When Saul realized that the LORD was with David and that his daughter Michal loved David, Saul became still more afraid of him, and he remained his enemy the rest of his days" (1 Sam. 18:28–29 NIV).

In his fear and anger, Saul crossed a line in his heart. He became so jealous and insecure that he turned on his son-in-law for the rest of his life. Saul spent the remainder of his days trying to take David out.

Now *that's* an in-law problem.

TURNING UP THE HEAT

Although David's relationship with his father-in-law was off to a rocky start, his bond with Jonathan continued to grow. But the heat was about to get turned up in both directions.

David found himself on the run and was forced to hide out in a city called Naioth. Unfortunately, Saul got wind of it and sent an army to bring back David's head on a platter.

"David fled from Naioth at Ramah and went to Jonathan and asked, 'What have I done? What is my crime? How have I wronged your father, that he is trying to kill me?'" (1 Sam. 20:1 NIV).

You can hear the panic in David's voice, can't you? He was scared, hiding out and on the run for his life. In a moment of frustration he pushed Jonathan, his best friend, for answers. Jonathan stood up for his friend and committed to find out what was going on. Then David reminded him of their covenant friendship: "David took an oath and said, 'Your father knows very well that I have found favor in your eyes'" (1 Sam. 20:3 NIV).

Jonathan reassured David that his father would surely tell him any plans he had against David, and then Jonathan made a huge statement to his friend: "Jonathan said to David, 'Whatever you want me to do, I'll do for you'" (1 Sam. 20:4 NIV).

Don't miss the magnitude of this statement. That was a huge

thing for Jonathan to say to David because Jonathan was the rightful heir to the throne. If anybody should have been submitting to anybody right here, it should have been David. He should have been submitting to Jonathan because he was Saul's son. But that was not what happened. Instead, it was a complete role reversal.

Without hesitating, Jonathan told David, "Whatever you want, I'm serving you now." In that moment, Jonathan got it. He understood how the hand of God had transferred from his father Saul's family to David's family. Together they talked about the events happening over the next few days, and they formulated their plan.

As it turned out, Saul was throwing a huge dinner party in the palace the following night, and both David and Jonathan were scheduled to be there. However, both men knew that when you showed up to a party at the palace, you never knew which Saul you were going to get.

Some nights you could get happy Saul, and everything would be fine. Other times you would get angry Saul, and things would get nutty really fast! David knew he couldn't take any chances. They devised a plan for Jonathan to warn David if Saul acted crazy. But before they went their separate ways, Jonathan took their friendship another step deeper and said, "Show me unfailing kindness like the LORD's kindness as long as I live, so that I may not be killed, and do not ever cut off your kindness from my family—not even when the LORD has cut off every one of David's enemies from the face of the earth" (1 Sam. 20:14–15 NIV).

In that moment, Jonathan owned up to the reality that eventually his family, the family tree of Saul, would be on the losing end. He knew when that happened, the whole country would want him, his children, and anyone else associated with him dead.

In the last brief moments before Jonathan headed back to the palace, he said to David, "Promise me you will remember me and my family, no matter what!" Jonathan understood all too well that when David became king, the family of Saul should be eradicated from the earth. It was the right thing for a new king to do. Don't take any chances on someone from Saul's family wanting revenge or taking a cheap shot. Just get rid of them during the power change. It was what had to happen.

"Jonathan made a covenant *with the house of David,* saying, 'May the LORD call David's enemies to account.' And Jonathan had David reaffirm his oath out of love for him, because he loved him as he loved himself" (1 Sam. 20:16–17 NIV, emphasis mine).

I want to point out that on this occasion Jonathan made a covenant not just with David but with the house of David. He didn't just make a man-to-man covenant; he made a covenant that would transcend generational lines. Jonathan wanted assurance that as long as David's family was on the earth, David would do Jonathan's family right!

In other words, they were saying to each other, "Regardless of what happens to us or how far apart we are, regardless of how much time or space separates us, here and now, we vow to take care of each other's family forever." Now that's friendship.

THAT KIND OF FRIEND

I grew up in a small town in rural northeast Indiana. We lived in the country, and my grandparents lived about two miles down the road from us in the same home my dad grew up in. Each time we'd visit my grandparents, I remember hearing my dad, Harold, tell stories about his friends playing sports in the yard and going on adventures in the fields around their little home.

When my grandfather died in 1999, our family went back to that little house my dad had grown up in to share a meal and be together for the afternoon. As we were finishing our meal, there was a knock on the door. My aunt answered the door and escorted a man in a suit into the dining room. My cousins and I didn't recognize the man. However, my dad, upon seeing him enter the room, stood to his feet and, with tears in his eyes, went immediately to him and hugged him.

After a long embrace, the man turned to our family seated there and said, "My name is John, and Harold and I were childhood friends." Turning back to my dad, he continued, "I live in Pennsylvania now, but when I heard your father had died, I knew I had to come." When I heard the man say that, I was blown away. What kind of friend books a flight within a few days, to an out-of-the-way place like my hometown, for the funeral of the father of a friend he hasn't seen in thirty years? Apparently, a good one.

I have never forgotten seeing that man walk into my grandparents' house that day. And I have often been challenged about the friendships in my life. We live in a world that emphasizes shallow, surface-level relationships. But God has a few relationships in each person's life that are meant to go much deeper than that. David and Jonathan had one. My father had one. And I'm thankful to have a few in my life.

BACK TO THE DINNER PARTY

The next night Saul threw the dinner party, and during dessert, he noticed an empty seat next to his daughter Michal. "Where's your husband, David? I wanted to bless him tonight." Jonathan caught on to what was up and started covering for David, which enraged Saul.

Saul became so angry he actually called out Jonathan's mom. He raged, "You son of a perverse and rebellious woman!" (1 Sam. 20:30 NIV).

And in his anger, he threw a spear at his own son! Why was Saul so upset? Because he could see the writing on the wall. Jonathan's siding with David was a slap in the face to his authority and their family. It was the equivalent of declaring defeat.

In that moment, Jonathan recognized his father was intent to kill David. Jonathan's covenant with David got ramped up yet another level. He was suddenly endangering his own life for the sake of his friend. In that moment, Jonathan became keenly aware that his friendship with David would be very costly.

FROM BOOK 1 TO BOOK 2

At the end of the first book of Samuel, several years later, the army of Israel—with Saul and Jonathan at the helm—was fighting a battle against the Philistines. The battle became so fierce that both King Saul and Jonathan lost their lives to the Philistines that day.

As the book of 1 Samuel ends and the book of 2 Samuel begins, David received the news of the deaths of his king and his best friend. The first chapter of 2 Samuel describes David mourning the loss of his friendship. It is one of the most gut-wrenching, heartfelt chapters in all of Scripture.

A STRANGE TWIST

After the days of mourning passed, David was anointed king and began leading the nation of Israel in a positive direction, and God began blessing him. Just a few chapters in, David was living the dream. He was on top of the world. He had made it. Beautiful home. Great view from the Oval Office. Everything was good. From shepherd to king, he had officially reached the pinnacle of his life and his kingdom's destiny!

Then the most amazing thing happened. Somewhere deep inside the heart of this king who had it all, he began to feel a void. On his lunch hour, with feet propped up on his desk, in the midst of a scene where David was enjoying his success, he asked a seemingly absurd question of a servant.

"David asked, 'Is there anyone still left of the house of Saul to whom I can show kindness for Jonathan's sake?'" (2 Sam. 9:1 NIV).

What? Why would David be asking this question? In keeping with protocol, the armies of Israel would have set out to eliminate the entire family of Saul when David became king. It was right to get rid of everyone who could pose a threat to the new guy. But King David asked the servant anyway.

NO RIGHT ANSWER

Now put yourself in the servant's sandals for a second. He was probably thinking, *What are you talking about? We've all been busting our tails to get rid of them for you! Now you want to know if anyone is left?* His next thought was, *There's no right answer here. Either way I answer, I lose.* Then the servant remembered one guy.

"As it turns out, there is a servant named Ziba who worked for Saul and is still around. But seriously, King David, why are you bringing up this bad chapter in our history? Don't you remember Saul chased you around for years and tried to kill you?"

So Ziba came to the palace. "Now there was a servant of Saul's household named Ziba. They summoned him to appear before David, and the king said to him, 'Are you Ziba?'" (2 Sam. 9:2 NIV). Imagine what he must have been thinking. Remember, David's people had just spent the last several years trying to get rid of anybody remotely connected with Saul. When Ziba got the call to come to the new king's office, he was probably thinking, *Oh no, they found me! I'm dead!* But consider what he said: "'At your service,' he replied" (2 Sam. 9:2 NIV).

Then David had a question for him. "The king asked, 'Is there no one still alive from the house of Saul to whom I can show God's kindness?'" (2 Sam. 9:3 NIV).

Much to the surprise of everyone, David asked the question not because he wanted to exact revenge. It was just the opposite. "Ziba answered the king, 'There is still a son of Jonathan; he is lame in both feet'"(2 Sam. 9:3 NIV).

Ziba, Saul's servant, probably breathed a huge sigh of relief when he heard the word *kindness* come out of David's mouth. He told the king one son of Jonathan's was still living, but he had a physical disability. Most probably the only reason they hadn't taken this guy out was that he was lame in both feet. In other words, according to their society, he was worthless. He was a lame underdog named Mephibosheth (Ma-phi-bo-sheth).

King David inquired a little deeper: "'Where is he?' the king asked. Ziba answered, 'He is at the house of Makir son of Ammiel in Lo Debar.' So King David had him brought from Lo Debar" (2 Sam. 9:4–5 NIV).

WHAT A CRAZY SCENE!

I imagine this scene like a movie. David, this good-looking, powerful young ruler, calling for a cultural throwaway. What a clash of worlds! What a collision of ideologies! David sitting on his throne while several strong men carry in a lame guy named Mephibosheth. Imagine what the palace guards must have been thinking.

You can also imagine what Mephibosheth must have been thinking: *They found me. I thought I had a good hiding place. I thought I had officially flown under the radar, but they've found me. And now King David himself probably wants to take me out.*

Can you imagine the fear he must have felt? Being utterly worthless to society *and* being from the wrong family. Now he was being carried in before the new king to be done away with by the king's own hand. But the story wasn't over yet.

> When Mephibosheth son of Jonathan, the son of Saul, came to David, he bowed down to pay him honor.
> David said, "Mephibosheth!" (2 Sam. 9:6 NIV)

When David saw this lame man carried in that day, he didn't see a refugee from the wrong family tree. He didn't see a throwaway or a fugitive. In that moment, David had a flashback of Mephibosheth crawling around as a toddler at his best friend Jonathan's feet. David called out his name because he was surprised and happy to see his friend's son! In the eyes of Mephibosheth, David saw Jonathan's eyes. In his smile, he saw his friend's smile. In his voice was his friend's voice. Mephibosheth, not knowing what to expect in this exchange, responded formally: "'At your service,' he replied" (2 Sam. 9:6 NIV).

But David wanted none of that. After all, this young man wasn't just anybody. This lame underdog was more special to him than anyone could possibly know. "'Don't be afraid,' David said to him, 'for I will surely show you kindness for the sake of your father Jonathan. I will restore to you all the land that belonged to your grandfather Saul, and you will always eat at my table'" (2 Sam. 9:7 NIV).

David wanted Mephibosheth to know that "once upon a time, your dad and I were close. Really. Really. Close. Your dad put his life on the line for me. And I will never forget the covenant we made. Years ago, before you were even born, your dad was my best friend." But Mephibosheth didn't grasp what the king said. "Mephibosheth bowed down and said, 'What is your servant, that you should notice a dead dog like me?'" (2 Sam. 9:8 NIV).

Mephibosheth couldn't get past himself. He saw himself as an underdog in the most literal sense of the word. He called himself a dead dog. The society around him saw him as a throwaway, a nuisance, a nothing. And that was just how he saw himself.

Hearing that, King David called in Saul's servant Ziba again:

> Then the king summoned Ziba, Saul's steward, and said to him, "I have given your master's grandson everything that belonged to Saul and his family. You and your sons and your servants are to farm the land for him and bring in the crops, so that your master's grandson may be provided for. And Mephibosheth, grandson of your master, will always eat at my table." (2 Sam. 9:9–10 NIV)

Did you catch that? David gave everything that ever belonged to Saul to Mephibosheth. And he commanded Ziba, his sons, and all his servants to farm the land for Mephibosheth, thirty-five of them in all! In one fell swoop, David picked up this unimaginable underdog and provided for him for the rest of his life. Complete rights of sonship, forever! David wanted him to have a seat at the king's table for the rest of his life. "So Mephibosheth ate at David's table like one of the king's sons" (2 Sam. 9:11 NIV).

WHY WOULD DAVID DO THAT?

If you're anything like me, you're probably asking why right about now. Why would this king, who clearly had more important things to do, go out of his way to make this kind of provision for a lame, dead dog throwaway? Why go to the trouble and expense? Why take on the burden? Why bother?

For David, the answer was simple: once upon a time, he had been friends with Mephibosheth's dad. They had a bond that transcended earthly logic and understanding.

WE CAN RELATE

You and I aren't much different from Mephibosheth. All of us have been born into the human race, and this sin thing is in all of us. Truth is, because God is a just God, we, the human race, deserve to be eradicated, just like Saul's family.

But once upon a time, someone from David's family offered friendship to us. David's great-grandson, forty-two generations later, was named Jesus. And Jesus dared to be friends with us, a human race full of lame underdogs.

Jesus came to this earth so you and I, dead dog, underdog sinners, could be brought up from our hiding places to the table of the King. Jesus came so you and I could be treated as sons and daughters of the King for the rest of our lives.

Maybe you've often considered yourself unworthy to sit at the King's table. Maybe you've been tempted to count yourself out or write yourself off. You are no different from Mephibosheth! A

King came to the earth so you could be redeemed and connected to him and be seated at his table forever. My prayer is that you will let that mindset sink in to the deepest part of your being right now.

> A King came to the earth so you could be redeemed and connected to him and be seated at his table forever.

Knowing who you are and how you've been redeemed has the power to change your life forever. Mephibosheth was an unimaginable underdog with the wrong connections, but he experienced one of the greatest acts of love in all of Scripture. May we forever live in the reality of the magnitude of our connection as well.

TheUnderdogsBook.com/ch6

**SCAN HERE FOR BONUS CONTENT ABOUT
"THE RIGHT CONNECTIONS."**

UNDERDOG EXCUSE #7

"My Resources Are Too Scarce"
(GIDEON)

{
Get up! The LORD has given the
Midianite camp into your hands.
JUDGES 7:15 NIV
}

IN DECEMBER 2010, WE FINALLY HAD THE PERMITS IN hand to begin work on our church's first permanent location. After nine years of being portable and growing our church to about one thousand people, God was finally giving us our first home. Now we just needed to gut the 14,000-square-foot, twenty-five-year-old church building; add 6,000 square feet of new construction to it; and completely overhaul the entire ten acres of property—all before April 9. We had seventeen weeks to be in by Easter.

The odds were stacked against us in a big way. It was an underdog moment like we had never faced before. The game was on the line. If we missed the Easter deadline, we would forfeit the greatest opportunity of the entire calendar year to invite our city to be a part of what God was doing in our church. We were facing impossible odds, but we felt God was with us, and we trusted him to get us in by Easter.

FACING SIMILAR ODDS

In Judges 6, we find the story of an underdog who was facing a similar situation, only much more dire. The children of Israel, God's people in the Old Testament, had seen God deliver them from slavery in Egypt, but within a few years they were right back in the same situation they had been in for more than four hundred years. Only this time it was with a group called the Midianites.

Where we pick up the story, the Midianites were so ruthless that the Israelites were living in mountains, caves, and makeshift tents just to avoid their oppressors. It was a bad situation. The Midianites were bullying them and destroying their crops. The Midianites had stolen their dignity and their livelihood. Worst of all, they had stolen their hope.

SEEING DESPERATION FIRSTHAND

One of the greatest ministries of our church involves working with residents of low-income communities in our city. We have seen oppression like that of the Israelites firsthand. Unfortunately, the offender goes beyond a neighborhood bully; the offender is generational poverty.

This is not just true in our city; there are millions upon millions of underprivileged underdogs who have had a defeated mind-set transferred to them from previous generations across our nation and our world. It's a mind-set that says, "You'll never break out. Your world can never be different. There is no hope."

One of the reasons I'm so passionate about the underdogs message is that I can see in my mind the faces of the residents of our communities we serve. To see hopelessness in a mother, longing in a child, and frustration and anger in the men breaks my heart. That's why we do what we do as a church, and that's why the message of this book is so urgent and important to me.

If we can give just one of these underdogs hope that he can change his reality, it's all worth it. These underdogs are worth the sacrifice. They are worth fighting for. They are worth so much more than they know.

TURNING TO GOD FOR HELP

God's people found themselves living under the oppressive hands of the Midianites. So they did the only thing they knew to do: they cried out to the Lord for help. Maybe, just maybe, God would intervene on their behalf. "Midian so impoverished the Israelites that they cried out to the LORD for help" (Judg. 6:6 NIV).

Thankfully, we serve a God who has a sweet spot in his heart for underdogs and particularly underprivileged underdogs. We serve a God who fights for the underdog. And boy, was he ever about to fight for the underdogs in this story. "When the Israelites cried out to the LORD because of Midian, he sent them a prophet" (Judg. 6:7–8 NIV).

Whenever people are in trouble, God's answer is often to find a leader to step in and change their plight. Let me say that again because I want you to get it:

> WHENEVER PEOPLE ARE IN TROUBLE, GOD'S
> ANSWER IS OFTEN TO FIND A LEADER TO
> STEP IN AND CHANGE THEIR PLIGHT.

An underdog named Gideon was God's answer. "When the angel of the LORD appeared to Gideon, he said, 'The LORD is with you, mighty warrior'" (Judg. 6:12 NIV).

Did you catch what God called him? A mighty warrior! Seriously? Here's a guy who had been living an impoverished, oppressed reality for the last seven years. So when it came to feeling like a mighty warrior, Gideon didn't. He saw himself as an underdog.

PUSHBACK

"Pardon me, my Lord," Gideon replied, "if the LORD is with us, why has all this happened to us? Where are all his wonders that our ancestors told us about when they said, 'Did not the LORD

bring us up out of Egypt?' But now the LORD has abandoned
us and given us into the hand of Midian." (Judg. 6:13 NIV)

I love Gideon's pushback right here. His question is legitimate, isn't it? "If life is supposed to be so good, why are things
so bad? If we are supposed to be your people and you're supposed to be our God, then, Lord, with all due respect, what
went wrong?"

Gideon's heart was in the right place in asking God
those questions. What he saw in reality didn't match what
the angel of the Lord was saying to him. In that moment, he
didn't feel like a mighty warrior. He felt like an underdog! He
and the entire nation felt like slaves all over again. Defeated.
Discouraged. Hopeless. But God was about to inspire this
defeated underdog.

Maybe you've felt the same way. Your heart is burdened for
some need, some issue, some wrong needing to be right. But
you've hesitated to step up and do something about it because
you don't *feel* like the mighty warrior you think it will take to
get the job done. Gideon didn't feel like being the man, but
God felt differently about him. And the same is true with you.

You are no longer allowed to let your circumstances keep
you from doing something great for God. Your circumstances
may tell you that you are a slave, abandoned, and a nobody,
but God says you are a mighty warrior. You are the one God
is choosing to right the wrong. We don't live by our feelings;
we live by our faith. "The LORD turned to him and said, 'Go
in the strength you have and save Israel out of Midian's hand.
Am I not sending you?'" (Judg. 6:14 NIV).

God said to Gideon, "I've put within your power everything you need to defeat the enemy, not because you are good enough, strong enough, or talented enough. Not because you have enough power or troops or weapons, but simply because you + me = a majority!" Let me say that again because you must get that! We serve a God who says,

$$\text{You} + \text{Me} = \text{A Majority}$$

NATURAL VS. SPIRITUAL

"'Pardon me, my lord,' Gideon replied, 'but how can I save Israel? My clan is the weakest in Manasseh, and I am the least in my family'" (Judg. 6:15 NIV).

When Gideon looked through the lens of his natural eyes, he couldn't see it. He didn't have the strength, he wasn't from the right family, and in an honest moment like this, he was even willing to admit he was the scrawniest of his entire family. Gideon pushed back because what he saw in the natural didn't line up with what he wanted to feel in the spiritual.

Maybe you can relate to Gideon in that regard. Maybe you've always had a dream to break the mold that was set for you by your family or your neighborhood. Maybe you've always wanted your life to be different than it has been up to now. But every time you've dared to dream of what could be, the reality of what you see in the natural has been like a bucket of water on the flame in your heart. What's outside doesn't match what's inside.

MISMATCH

Sarah and I felt the original tug to Fort Myers, Florida, when we were still teenagers. My parents took us to southwest Florida on a spring break vacation while we were just dating in high school. It was March 1993, and when the plane landed, I turned to my then-girlfriend and said, "Let's start a church here someday."

In the nine years between the initial burden to plant a church in southwest Florida and the time we moved in 2002, I can remember vividly saying to the Lord, "God, what does a small-town kid from Auburn, Indiana, have to offer people in Fort Myers, Florida?" I was nothing special. I felt inadequate. I felt mismatched with my calling.

But the one thing Gideon and I had in common was that we were available. Wherever, however, and whenever God wanted to lead us, we were willing to follow. For me, it was to southwest Florida, and for Gideon, it was into battle with the Midianites. It doesn't mean there weren't moments of pushback, which is precisely where Gideon found himself. But God wanted to reassure Gideon that he had his back. "The Lord answered, 'I will be with you, and you will strike down all the Midianites'" (Judg. 6:16 NIV).

God needed Gideon to get past his own doubt if God was going to be able to help him through it.

ASKING FOR A SIGN

"Gideon replied, 'If now I have found favor in your eyes, give me a sign that it is really you talking to me. Please do not go away until I come back and bring my offering and set it before you'" (Judg. 6:17–18 NIV).

Gideon wanted proof! He was like, "Okay, God, if this is really you and not just the pizza I ate last night, stay here while I go and get a sacrifice to offer to you." And much to Gideon's surprise, God was like, "Okay, I'll stay." So Gideon ran off, cooked up an offering, and brought it back. Sure enough, God received it, and he said in response, "Peace! Do not be afraid. You are not going to die" (Judg. 6:23 NIV).

I love this part of the story for a couple of reasons. First, because Gideon asked for a sign. When we feel that God might be in something, it's important to know that God is perfectly fine with us asking him to give us confirmation. God doesn't regard our asking for a sign as a lack of faith or trust in him. He is perfectly fine with us seeking confirmation as we step out in faith for him.

Second, I love that the Lord's response to Gideon after he received the sacrifice was peace. When we are stepping out in a big way for God, I am a firm believer in following the peace. There have been so many times when I have lacked peace in my heart but made a decision anyway. I regretted it every time. Only after the fact, when I reflected on the decision, did I realize I didn't have peace from the outset. Consequently, this has become a part of the language of our church and of our family personally.

THIRD-GRADE PEACE

When my younger son was in third grade, he was struggling in his class at school. He is a good student but was surrounded by a few kids who were making his school experience less than enjoyable.

One night Sarah and I sat down with him and told him we thought he should think about changing schools, which is a big deal for a third grader. Naturally, he was nervous and unsure, but Sarah reassured him that if God was in it, he would know because he would feel peace about it.

A few weeks later he went for a shadow day at the new school. Heading into the school, Sarah prayed with him and asked God to give him peace if this was where he was supposed to be. Nervously stepping out of the car, he was met by a third-grade guide who led him into the unknown surroundings.

At the end of the day, when Sarah picked him up, he came running out to the car, jumped in, and shouted, "Mom, I've got the peace! I've got the peace!" Needless to say, he loved the new school, recognized several kids from our church, and was already bragging about his new classroom. Peace is a powerful thing. When you've got it, there's nothing like it, and when you don't, you'll know it.

Never underestimate the power of peace in the decision-making zone of your life. Maybe you're facing a decision right now and you don't have peace about it. Don't ignore that. Maybe you're in a dating relationship, and every time the conversation turns toward marriage, you don't feel peace. Don't ignore that. Maybe you're planning to make a major purchase, but you just don't feel peace about it. Whatever the situation, keep pressing in to God until you find that peace. You will save yourself a ton of heartache later if you follow the peace now.

DOING SOMETHING DRASTIC

After Gideon received his confirmation from the Lord, he did something drastic. He went straight into the center of town to a huge shrine of a false god and tore it down. He used the wood from the shrine as fuel for a huge fire. Talk about a way to get the city's attention! In order for his people to move away from where they were, Gideon knew they needed a shove in the right direction.

The result was that some town leaders wanted to kill him. Thankfully, his dad went to bat for him and held the crowd off long enough for Gideon to get them ready to attack their oppressors.

In every underdog story, the underdog never acts alone. There is always someone somewhere who makes a way or opens a door that would not otherwise be opened to him. When we step out for God and decide to be used by him, God will move the hands of the right people at the right time to make his plan succeed. Time after time, I have seen God move the hand of someone powerful in order to get done what needed to get done for his people.

I GET BY WITH A LITTLE HELP
FROM MY FRIEND

By February 2011, construction was moving along at a lightning-fast pace on our church building. It was miraculous to see the speed with which the construction crews were working. They had caught the vision, and the Easter deadline was becoming a reality. However, to stay on track, we needed to place the order for the sound equipment and furnishings to be ready for our grand opening.

When we went to the bank to access the $150,000 needed for the order, we were informed the money was in our account, but we would not be able to touch it until all the other construction loans had cleared. That meant the building would be ready for the grand opening, but there would be no sound system, no lighting, and no chairs.

Needless to say, I began making pretty desperate phone calls to some of my closest pastor friends across the country in an attempt to borrow $150,000. My logic: if we could get six churches to loan us $25,000 each for ninety days, we'd be all right. (After all, the money was in the bank. We just couldn't touch it.)

One call was to a close friend who pastors a great church. I explained the situation to him, and he told me he was headed into a meeting with his church board that night and would call me later if they could help. Sounded good to me. I hung up the phone, hopeful they would be able to loan us a portion of the money.

Around 10:30 p.m., Sarah and I were in our pajamas getting ready to call it a night when the phone rang. It was my friend. He told me he and his board had talked about our situation but also about how they were trying to launch a second campus for their church. So, needless to say, money was at a premium for them at that time as well. As he continued to talk, my heart began to sink a little bit.

He went on to tell me that after about twenty minutes of

conversation, they went to prayer for us and for their campus expansion. Then they asked God to speak. After about thirty minutes of prayer, the most conservative of all the board members raised his head and matter-of-factly said, "I think we should give Next Level Church the $150,000 for their building as a seed for what we need for ours."

All of the board members were instantly in agreement, and they voted a few minutes later to give our church the $150,000 we needed to complete our building! Not a loan. A gift! Needless to say, I was standing speechless in my pajamas in my bedroom! When I mouthed the words to Sarah, we both just lost it! We cried and laughed and screamed, and so did my friend. It was one of the biggest financial miracles I've ever seen in my life.

We finished the building in seventeen weeks, and within nine months, our church had doubled in size from just under one thousand people in weekly attendance to more than two thousand people every week. It was truly an underdog miracle of epic proportions! And it never would have been possible without someone making a way for us when there was no way.

Every underdog story includes such moments. Moments when we step out in honest faith, and God moves the hand of the right person at the right time and opens the door for us to do what God has called us to do.

ASKING FOR TWO MORE SIGNS

Gideon's next step was to assemble the army so they could take on the Midianites. He pulled together everyone he could find from the surrounding regions and came up with about 32,000 men. Not a bad number except that the army they were going up against was 135,000 men! I don't know where you come from, but where I come from we call those not very good odds.

Gideon was an under-resourced underdog. So he did what anyone would do when faced with those kinds of odds: he asked for another sign! Two of them, to be exact. "Gideon said to God, 'If you will save Israel by my hand as you have promised—look, I will place a wool fleece on the threshing floor. If there is dew only on the fleece and all the ground is dry, then I will know that you will save Israel by my hand, as you said'" (Judg. 6:36–37 NIV).

Gideon put a fleece before the Lord, and sure enough, God came through the next morning. The fleece was so wet he actually rang it out into a bowl. But before going to war in a one-on-four battle, Gideon asked God for one more proof: "If you're *really* in this, then reverse it. Let the ground be wet and the fleece be dry." Sure enough, God came through again.

Armed with that knowledge, Gideon had the confidence to take on the oppressors of his people. Little did he know, God was about to stack the deck yet again, but not in his favor.

DOUBTING, DRINKING, AND
DWINDLING NUMBERS

Early in the morning, . . . [Gideon] and all his men camped at the spring of Harod. The camp of Midian was north of them in the valley near the hill of Moreh. The LORD said to Gideon, "You have too many men. I cannot deliver Midian into their hands, or

Israel would boast against me, 'My own strength has saved me.'
Now announce to the army, 'Anyone who trembles with fear may
turn back and leave Mount Gilead.'" So twenty-two thousand
men left, while ten thousand remained. (Judg. 7:1–3 NIV)

Did you catch that? Just about the time Gideon was gaining
his confidence to go and fight as an under-resourced underdog,
God cut him off at the knees. God told him to let anyone who was
afraid go home. What? Isn't everybody afraid in a war where it's
four-on-one in favor of the bad guys? But thankfully, ten thousand men stayed. And the odds were thirteen to one. Surely this
was good enough for God to get the glory and for the people not
to take the credit, right? Wrong. "But the LORD said to Gideon,
'There are still too many men. Take them down to the water, and
I will thin them out for you there'" (Judg. 7:4 NIV).

"Perfect, let's make more of them go home, shall we, God?
Seriously, this is getting kind of ugly." But wait. It got worse. Watch
how God was going to decide who would stay and who would go.
It was not about who were the strongest or best warriors. No, it
came down to *how they got a drink of water!* "There the LORD told
him, 'Separate those who lap the water with their tongues as a dog
laps from those who kneel down to drink'" (Judg. 7:5 NIV).

Are you kidding me? The entire fate of their nation was
going to be determined by how a bunch of thugs drank from the
river? Surely God had a better idea than that! "Three hundred
of them drank from cupped hands, lapping like dogs. All the
rest got down on their knees to drink. The LORD said to Gideon,
'With the three hundred men that lapped I will save you'" (Judg.
7:6–7 NIV).

Okay, so God didn't even choose the 9,700; he chose the 300! Don't blow past this.

Think about it: 135,000 versus 300. For you Vegas bookies out there, that's 450 to 1 odds. For every soldier for the good guys, there were 366 bad guys. "So Gideon sent the rest of the Israelites home but kept the three hundred, who took over the provisions and trumpets of the others" (Judg. 7:8 NIV).

I do love this, though. Gideon at least held the line on making the face drinkers leave their backpacks and supplies with them. "We'll let you go back to camp, but you have to leave your gear with us. Trust me, I think we're going to need it."

DEFEATED MIND-SET

At this point, I have to ask, why would the other 31,700 soldiers agree to leave? There's no indicator anywhere in the story that they resisted Gideon or put up a fight to let them stay. Rather, we have every indication they took off as fast as they could and got out of there. Why? Didn't they want to defend themselves and fight for their families and for what was right?

No, they didn't! They didn't think they had a chance to win. So, rather than stand up for what was right, they had just resolved themselves that they were going to be slaves of the Midianites forever and that nothing would ever change for them. Their children would be stuck in this poverty just like they were. Their hopelessness was greater than their hope of changing their circumstances.

How sad. And the truly sad reality for me is how many people in our world have become resolved to the same conclusion.

Rather than believe there is a God who will fight for them and defend them and help them create the kind of change they long to see, they have shut down. They have given up hope that things could possibly be different for them or their children.

Listen, if that's you, I want you to know that attitude is not okay with me or, more importantly, with our God! If you can dream of a better reality for yourself or your children, I'm calling you, one underdog to another, to stand up and fight! It doesn't matter how high you think the odds are stacked against you. We serve a God who is fighting for you. You can do this! You can overcome whatever you are living under.

You can overcome whatever you are living under.

Get off the couch; make a determination that you and your future are worth fighting for. We need you. Your children need you. Our world needs you not to turn and run. You need to stand and fight for a better reality than you've been given up to this point. You may be the underdog, but you are serving the God of the underdogs who has a way of bringing freedom to the captives and victory to the underresourced.

Never forget that

$$You + God = A\ Majority$$

ONE LAST SHOT OF CONFIDENCE

Now the camp of Midian lay below him in the valley. During that night the LORD said to Gideon, "Get up, go down against the camp, because I am going to give it into your hands. If you are

afraid to attack, go down to the camp with your servant Purah and
listen to what they are saying." (Judg. 7:8–11 NIV)

In an effort to pump up Gideon one last time, God told him to sneak down to the camp of the Midianites and listen to what they were talking about. When Gideon and his servant got down there, they heard two soldiers talking about a dream they had and how the army of Israel demolished them. Upon hearing that, Gideon got all fired up and rushed back to mobilize his motley crew to take on the 135,000 enemy troops.

God has a way of keeping us motivated on the journey. He knows we need the encouragement along the way. Ever had one of those moments when just as you started to doubt what you were doing, God gave you a sign of confirmation that you were headed in the right direction? I certainly have. In fact, those small, subtle reminders along the way have kept me going during some of the darkest seasons of my underdog journey.

A note from a friend telling me that he believes in me. An encouraging e-mail or text just before I take the stage to speak. A timely word from my wife telling me she believes in me. Even a song on the radio that comes on at just the right time. Don't underestimate those small reminders. They're more than coincidence; they're the hand of God propelling you forward into all he's calling you to do.

THE FIGHT

When Gideon heard the dream and its interpretation, he bowed
down and worshiped. He returned to the camp of Israel and called

out, "Get up! The LORD has given the Midianite camp into your hands." Dividing the three hundred men into three companies, he placed trumpets and empty jars in the hands of all of them, with torches inside. (Judg. 7:15–16 NIV)

I'm sorry, what? He did what? He gave them what to fight with? Swords? Nope. Knives? Nah. Bazookas? Cannons? Horses? Shields? Bows? Nope. Nope. Nope. Nope. Nope. Gideon's grand plan to defeat the 135,000 Midianites was to use a musical instrument, a pickle jar, and a flashlight!

It's true. Not only was God giving them ridiculous odds, but he also wanted them to know that victory would not come by conventional wisdom. It would come from his hand. He was saying, "Don't be trusting in your swords and spears and ideas and schemes. Either trust me, or trust nothing."

When it comes to achieving victory in your life, God's not interested in bringing it to pass in the old familiar way. He's interested in setting it up so only he can get the glory. And trust me: with trumpets, pickle jars, and flashlights, it was definitely arranged so only he could get the glory! "'Watch me,' he told them. 'Follow my lead. When I get to the edge of the camp, do exactly as I do. When I and all who are with me blow our trumpets, then from all around the camp blow yours and shout, "For the LORD and for Gideon"'" (Judg. 7:17–18 NIV).

The plan was to surround them on three sides and then shout, blow the trumpets, smash the pickle jars, make bags of popcorn, and watch the action unfold in front of them. Simple enough, right? Sure, unless your entire family lineage is on the line. But they did it.

Gideon and the hundred men with him reached the edge of the camp at the beginning of the middle watch, just after they had changed the guard. They blew their trumpets and broke the jars that were in their hands. The three companies blew the trumpets and smashed the jars. Grasping the torches in their left hands and holding in their right hands the trumpets they were to blow, they shouted, "A sword for the LORD and for Gideon!" (Judg. 7:19–20 NIV)

Look what happened next; you can't make this stuff up: "When the three hundred trumpets sounded, the LORD caused the men throughout the camp to turn on each other with their swords" (Judg. 7:22 NIV).

God so confused the enemy that they started killing each other! You know how you get 300 men to defeat 135,000 men? Cause the 135,000 to fight each other while the 300 men stand around and watch. Brilliant! Only God could come up with that plan.

SAME GOD TODAY AS BACK THEN

What God can do for Gideon and his men, he can do for you! The same God who infused courage in the heart of an under-resourced underdog can infuse courage in your heart. If you're facing a situation that is less than God's best for you or your family, then rise up, underdog! Rise up, mighty warrior, and lead the change you want to see.

We serve a God whose heart is big for the underprivileged in our world today. And whenever we fight for them, we don't fight alone. We have a God who fights with us, and though the enemy may look like it has us outnumbered, we have a God who can confuse the enemy and cause them to turn on themselves.

So I'm calling all Gideon underdogs! No matter if you think you have the resources to succeed or not, you have a God who can take some band instruments, pickle jars, and flashlights and turn them into just the tools you need to defeat your enemy and step into the breakthrough you've always dreamed of.

CHAPTER 7 QR CODE (image)
**THEUNDERDOGSBOOK.COM/CH7
SCAN HERE FOR BONUS CONTENT ABOUT
"FACING A RESOURCE CHALLENGE."**

8

UNDERDOG EXCUSE #8

"My Chances Are Too Slim"

(ESTHER)

{

Who knows but that you have come to your
royal position for such a time as this?

ESTHER 4:14 NIV

}

I CAN STILL HEAR THE MUFFLED SOUND OF THE WOMAN'S
voice over the loudspeaker announcing the final boarding call
for the flight to Indiana. Both sets of parents were on that flight.
We were not. After a 1,300-mile road trip in a moving truck and
then three days on the beach with our whole family together, it
had all felt surreal and more like vacation than transition. Until
this moment.

For the first time in our lives, we were truly on our own. No friends. No family. Nobody nearby who could bail us out or catch us if we fell. Sarah and I were sobbing as we pushed the stroller with our eighteen-month-old son inside to the car my grandfather gave me when he died. Partly in sadness, partly in fear. As we pulled away from the airport that day, I said to Sarah, "I think we grew up a lot today."

What were we doing? We had no idea how to start a church! I didn't even have a job. I was responsible for our family and our future. All our chips were on the table. We were all in, but the odds of winning seemed razor thin. In that moment, we were more than a little aware of just how stacked against us the deck really was.

In the Old Testament, we find the story of an underdog who felt the same way. In the land of Susa, there was a king named Xerxes. He was an okay guy with a bad leadership style. King Xerxes was married to Queen Vashti. One day, after a long weekend of partying and trying to look cool in front of a bunch of his boys, the king asked the queen to do a little dance in front of everybody.

Queen Vashti refused to be the halftime entertainment, and that didn't sit well with the king. He was humiliated in front of his drinking buddies. So, in his embarrassment, he wouldn't let the queen off the hook. He called in a bunch of his attorney friends, and they began playing out worst-case scenarios.

They reasoned, "If she gets away with this, we will have an all-out revolt from every woman in the country thinking she can do the same thing to her husband." They concluded that if they didn't come down hard on Vashti, "there will be no end of disrespect and discord" (Esther 1:18 NIV). So the king and all his buddies banned her from the palace forever.

THE SEARCH FOR A NEW QUEEN BEGINS

After Vashti was removed from the palace, they assembled a group of possible replacement candidates: young ladies who were beautiful and smart. Among the women was a young girl named Esther. And as it turned out, Esther was an underdog.

If anyone should have been out of the running for doing something great with her life, it was Esther. If anyone had a slim chance at becoming queen, it was Esther. The deck was truly stacked against her from the start. After all, her parents had died while she was young, thus making her a throwaway to her society. Thankfully, her cousin Mordecai didn't see her that way. Mordecai chose not to give up on her. He saw the beauty and potential inside her. He took her in and raised her as his own.

Maybe you can identify with Esther in feeling that your chances are slim. Perhaps you've had a dream in your heart to become something great, but you've felt that your chances were too slim to even try. Don't count yourself out too quickly. God had a purpose for Esther's life, and he has a purpose for your life as well.

FROM WORST TO FIRST

One of the great traditions of our family is attending the Indianapolis 500 auto race each Memorial Day weekend in Indianapolis. My dad and I began attending the race when I was in fifth grade, and today we still have the same eight seats on the front straightaway across from the start-finish line. It's an annual event I wouldn't miss for the world. It takes a bit more work these days to pull together because I take both of my sons and we fly in from Florida, but it is always worth the time and energy to create the memories the race provides.

Through the years people have occasionally asked me, "Isn't it boring just watching a bunch of cars go in circles all afternoon?" My answer, and the answer of my kids, is always, "No! Are you kidding?" Every year is unique, exciting, and memorable. Each year it seems the race offers a unique story line. In 2012, something particularly memorable took place during the five-hundred-mile race.

Early in the race, Dario Franchitti, a two-time winner then, was hit by another car while pulling into his pit stop. His car flew past his pit box, hit a tire, and spun backward in the pit lane. Not only was it a dangerous situation, but it was extremely costly in terms of track position. By the time Franchitti left the pit lane, he was in last place in the race.

Franchitti, however, didn't give up. Instead, he fought his way back to the front of the field. Dodging another crash on the final lap, he won his third Indy 500, a feat accomplished by only seven other drivers in the history of the race! If he had given up too soon, he would have forfeited becoming one of the elite drivers in the history of his sport.

If the start of your race hasn't been what you hoped it would be, don't give up! There are still a lot of laps to go. No matter how far back in the field you may feel you are, God is still at work. The race isn't over yet. Keep pressing the gas pedal; don't give up. You have something to offer. There's more in you than meets the eye.

INTANGIBLES

As if having a rough childhood weren't enough, Esther was also from the wrong nationality. Esther's family was of Jewish descent, meaning she would have been treated like an outsider, or worse, like a slave in those days. But her cousin Mordecai didn't let that stop her. He encouraged her to stay in the running for queen as long as she could. Mordecai saw something in her that others couldn't see. Esther was an underdog with slim chances, but she had something the other girls didn't have: intangibles. "When the turn came for Esther . . . to go to the king, she asked for nothing other than what Hegai, the king's eunuch who was in charge of the harem, suggested. And Esther won the favor of everyone who saw her" (Esther 2:15 NIV).

We don't know exactly what it was about Esther that made her stand out, but the Bible makes it clear: something about her made her special. Her uniqueness gave her favor.

The same is true for you. Your uniqueness makes you stand out from everyone else. Your uniqueness won't look like Esther's, and it shouldn't. You are uniquely designed for the destiny God has in mind for you. Let me say that again because you must get it:

YOU ARE UNIQUELY DESIGNED FOR THE
DESTINY GOD HAS IN MIND FOR YOU.

Stop trying to look like everyone else. You don't have to fit the mold of what everyone else says is cool. You be you. We don't need another someone else. We need the best version of you!

God's given you unique intangibles that set you apart from everybody else.

Historically, those whom God used in a great way have always been unique. They haven't fit society's mold. They have intangibles. And so do you. God wants to use your life in a big way, and he's going to use your intangibles to do it. Esther's intangibles positioned her to do great things.

CHOSEN

So Esther was brought before the king, and he made his choice for his new queen: "[He] was attracted to Esther more than to any of the other women, and she won his favor and approval" (Esther 2:17 NIV).

The king chose Esther. But I think it's worth pointing out one important distinction here. Esther was chosen by *the* King long before she was chosen by King Xerxes. Yes, Esther found favor with the earthly king Xerxes, but before she was ever chosen by him, God, our heavenly King, had put his hand of favor on her. Esther's earthly favor was directly linked to her heavenly favor.

> Though you may feel like nothing special on the outside, you are chosen on the inside.

If you feel like an underdog with slim chances, know that you have been chosen by a heavenly King. You may consider the circumstances of your life and feel that you are nothing special, just another in a long line of sameness. Nothing could be further from the truth! Though you may feel like nothing special on the outside, you are chosen on the inside.

The Creator of the universe has put his hand on you to accomplish great things for him. He wants to use your life in a way that he will use no one else's. You are a prized possession to him. He has favored and approved you. Don't shrink back from that; instead, lean into it. That's where your greatness comes from. Not from your strength, talent, or qualifications but from the hand of God on you. Esther had it, and so do you. A heavenly King has chosen you, and that sets you up to be chosen by earthly kings in the future.

> God has a way of arranging circumstances to create what I call "only-God" coincidences.

In Esther's time, God knew the threat about to come. He needed someone in the right place at the right time to head off disaster for his people. And the same is true in your life. Trust his timing and provision. You are right where he needs you to be. God has a way of arranging circumstances to create what I call "only-God" coincidences.

"ONLY-GOD" COINCIDENCES

After the king chose Esther to be the new queen, it just so happened (only-God coincidence) that Mordecai was sitting outside the king's gate when he overheard two guys conspiring to assassinate the king. Of course, he immediately told

Esther, and she went straight to the king to warn him. After his guards investigated the matter, the two men were hanged. Crisis diverted. Oh, but it gets better. Fast-forward five years.

ALL IS NOT WELL IN THE PALACE

After Esther had enjoyed five years of palace living, everything seemed to be going well for her. Esther was used to living there, the king seemed relatively satisfied with his life, and Mordecai had worked out his schedule so he could see Esther daily to give her advice and encouragement. Life was moving along just fine until one of the king's officials, Haman, decided he had it in for Mordecai.

He didn't just have it in for Mordecai; he had it in for the entire Jewish population living in the land. Haman wanted to kill Mordecai and all of the Jews, and he had the power and position to do it. One day, January 13 to be exact, he went in to see the king and convinced him to sign a law that would put every Jew living in the entire nation to death on December 13.

Obviously, when the heralds began delivering the news throughout the countryside about this new law, people were alarmed. After all, if someone didn't stop it, the entire Jewish race would be destroyed.

In a moment of desperation, Mordecai went to his cousin, the queen, and begged her to get involved in the situation. Mordecai pleaded with her to go before the king and convince him to change his mind. But that was easier said than done. In those days, queens didn't interfere with the decisions of kings. To do so was disrespectful and deserving of death. (Remember, the last queen was thrown out for not dancing at a weekend party!)

MOMENT OF DECISION

Esther found herself at a point of decision. She had a comfortable life. All she had to do was not make waves for herself, and she would live in the palace for the rest of her life. Nice clothes, fine foods, beautiful accommodations. She had a guarantee of a good life. Keep her mouth shut, fly under the radar, be pretty, and she would win.

Except that's not why she was there.

At the news of the king's edict to kill the Jews, Mordecai had to try to remind her of why God had put her in that position at that time:

Do not think that because you are in the king's house you alone of all the Jews will escape. For if you remain silent at this time, relief and deliverance for the Jews will arise from another place, but you and your father's family will perish. And who knows but that you have come to your royal position for such a time as this? (Esther 4:13–14 NIV)

Queen Esther was faced with an underdog decision of epic proportions. Would she choose the safe route, which might not be safe in the end, or would she choose the greater risk and potential greater reward?

SAME KIND OF CHOICE

As you read the pages in the late stages of this book, you are faced with the same choice as Esther. There stands before you, underdog, an opportunity to make a difference somewhere, with someone, in some way. I believe the Spirit of God has been opening your eyes as you've read the pages of this book to the void your life is designed to fill. It may not seem on the surface to be as magnificent as Esther's situation, but don't count it out too quickly.

What are the implications if you don't step in? What group will not be led? What organization will not be created? What idea will not be set forth? What business will not be started? What jobs will not be generated in the coming years? What lives will not be changed? Who are we to say the dreams of God in our hearts are too small for us to give our lives for them? Who knows? Maybe God is at work.

"WHO KNOWS BUT . . ."

Three words stand out to me in Mordecai's plea to Esther. They are *who knows but*. When Mordecai appealed to her, he could not make any guarantees. He didn't know how the situation would end. He hadn't read the end of the story. If she went to the king, he could not promise things would end well for her or for their people.

But Mordecai's faith was high. He was able to say, "Who knows but . . ." In other words, we may not know the outcome of this situation, but we do know we can't make a shot we never take. Hockey great Wayne Gretzky said, "You miss 100 percent of the shots you never take." Something like that must have been going through Mordecai's mind that day.

And the same is true for us. Listen, if you have the conversation with your boss, I can't tell you how it will end up. If you ask the girl out, I can't promise she will say yes. If you apply for the position, there's no guarantee you'll get accepted. The odds may be stacked against you. The margins may very well be slim. All I can say is, "Who knows but . . ."

Who knows but God might just come through on your behalf! Who knows but God may show up at just the right time and pull out a miracle on your behalf. Who knows but God could deliver you in the nick of time. Who knows but you miss 100 percent of the shots you never take. Who knows but God?

EVEN IF IT DOESN'T WORK

During the fall of 2001, after I had resigned from my position and we were trying to raise money for the church plant in Florida, I had lunch with a longtime friend. He graciously sat through my pitch about the church and asked a few questions. Then, as our lunch was coming to a close, he looked across the table and said, "You know, Matt, I think it's great. And hey, even if it doesn't work, at least you can say you tried. Right?"

Even if it doesn't work? I was crushed. This guy had been a friend and mentor to me for years. So much of what I had learned, I had learned from him. To hear someone like him doubt our chances made me doubt as well. It was years before I told Sarah about what he said to me that day over lunch.

I'm so glad that even when others doubted, God gave us a "who knows but God" kind of faith. Listen, if there are doubting voices in your life, move away from them. Like Esther, you have no time for naysayers. You've got people to save and a world to change. Who knows but God?

ESTHER'S DECISION

After hearing Mordecai's appeal, Esther asked him and all the other Jews living around the palace to fast and pray for her for three days. After the three days were up, she went to the king's chamber. When she passed by the door, the king noticed her and invited her in. Being happy to see her, he promised to give her anything she asked for, up to half the kingdom.

Rather than give him an answer right then and there, Esther asked the king to come to a banquet. Thrilled at the idea, he invited someone else to accompany him. Haman: the very person who had convinced the king to kill all the Jews.

When they got to the banquet, the king once again asked her what she wanted, and rather than tell him, she invited him to another banquet the next day. I don't know if this was a tactic to try and get rid of Haman or what, but either way, Esther decided to put off her request for another twenty-four hours.

As if things couldn't get any more dramatic, on the way home that night, Haman saw Mordecai outside the palace. At the very sight of him, he got so angry that by the time his family and friends finished dinner, they had devised a plan to construct a seventy-five-foot-tall gallows to hang Mordecai on the next morning! Talk about tense.

MEANWHILE, BACK IN THE PALACE

While Haman and his cronies were building a huge hangman set throughout the night, back in the palace, the king was having trouble sleeping. In an attempt to get drowsy, the king decided to catch up on some news of the kingdom. A servant began reading some of the newspapers from a few years ago to him. In the process, they ran across the story of Mordecai breaking up the plot to assassinate the king. Upon hearing that, the king asked if anything had ever been done to honor Mordecai for what he did on the king's behalf.

When he found out nothing had been done, King Xerxes decided to ask someone what to do. As the sun was coming up across the courtyard, he saw Haman coming in for work, and he immediately called him in. When the king asked Haman what should be done for someone the king wanted to honor, Haman immediately thought he must be talking about him, and so Haman suggested the most extravagant of rewards.

Haman's idea was to give the hero a game-worn jersey or robe from the king and a game-used horse ridden by the king. Then he suggested they parade the hero around the entire city with someone announcing how great the person was to everyone in town. What happened next is priceless: "'Go at once,' the king commanded Haman. 'Get the robe and the horse and do just as you have suggested for Mordecai the Jew, who sits at the king's gate'" (Esther 6:10 NIV).

Boom! Can you imagine how sick Haman must have felt? After all, he stayed up all night building a gallows to hang Mordecai on that morning. Instead, he had to get him and be the guy to yell out how great Mordecai was!

BANQUET #2

After the parade for Mordecai, the king and Haman headed in to the banquet that Esther had prepared for them. After a few glasses of wine, the king once again asked Esther what she wanted. It was her moment. It was her chance. And this orphan underdog went for it. She took the shot!

> Then Queen Esther answered, "If I have found favor with you, Your Majesty, and if it pleases you, grant me my life—this is my petition. And spare my people—this is my request. For I and my people have been sold to be destroyed, killed and annihilated." (Esther 7:3–4 NIV)

When the king heard her request, he was blown away. He asked her who was behind this horrible plot, and she pointed at Haman and called him out. "Esther said, 'An adversary and enemy! This vile Haman'" (Esther 7:6 NIV).

Hearing that, the king stormed out, disgusted and sick. When Haman realized his popularity points with the king just went to an all-time low, he fell at Esther's feet and began begging her for mercy. My, how the tables turned! Suddenly, this once powerful abuser of people was powerless before Esther the underdog!

When the king returned, he was told of Haman's gallows and of his intention to hang Mordecai on them. Then, in a moment of poetic irony of divine proportions, the king ordered Haman to be hanged on the very gallows he built to destroy Mordecai.

Esther told the king she and Mordecai were related, and the king immediately promoted him to serve in the king's palace alongside him and the queen. Mordecai was given a royal robe and a signet ring, meaning he had the full weight and authority of the king. Esther and Mordecai ended up being the ones who wrote the follow-up decree canceling the law to destroy the Jews. The new edict gave the people of God more rights and power than they had ever had. Esther, the underdog with slim odds, was the hero who saved the people of God from annihilation and destruction.

THE RESULT

Because of Esther's courage in the face of slim odds, the Bible says many people in the land put their faith in God. The people of God were saved that day because of the courage of one orphaned underdog who yielded her life to God's great purpose. Although Esther's chances were slim, God's plan was perfect.

If you find yourself in a situation similar to Esther's, take heart. It's easy to look at your present circumstances and want to give up. Don't! The story isn't over yet. Far from it! You have no idea what God has laid out for you five years from now. Or ten or twenty.

Looking back, over a decade removed from dropping off our parents at the airport and beginning our new life here in Florida, I am amazed! I could not have written the story God has allowed us to live. The thousands of lives changed, the churches planted, the leaders trained, and the impact made are truly mind-blowing. I'm so glad we didn't quit when the odds looked dauntingly against us.

Esther was unique, prepared, and willing to be used by God, and because she was, God used her in a great way to save his people. If Esther had not responded to his call, the people of God would have been annihilated, and there would have been no bloodline for Jesus to come from. Esther's life and decision were of eternal importance to the entire human race. We have salvation because of one underdog's courage to step up in the face of impossible odds.

Now it's your turn.

CHAPTER 8 QR CODE (image)
**THEUNDERDOGSBOOK.COM/CH8
SCAN HERE FOR BONUS CONTENT
ABOUT "BEING COURAGEOUS."**

UNDERDOG EXCUSE #9

"I'm Insecure"

(MOSES)

{
Moses said, "Pardon your servant,
Lord. Please send someone else."
EXODUS 4:13 NIV
}

WHEN WE TALK ABOUT BEING USED BY GOD AND LIVING our destiny, often the excuse that holds us back the most is insecurity. As we begin the final chapter of this book, we must tackle this all-important subject of facing our insecurities. After all, most of the time we are our own worst enemies. If the world doesn't defeat us, too often we defeat ourselves. Our insecurities keep us from becoming everything God wants us to be. They keep us from living our destiny.

THE "PERFECT" EXCUSE

One of the tricks the Devil uses to sabotage our lives is to get us to believe that the people God uses have reached a level of perfection that we have not. We see people being used by God, and we think they are doing so because they have it all together, have no

Most of the time, we are our own worst enemies.

problems, or have somehow attained a place in their relationship with God where they no longer struggle. It's almost as if they are made of a plastic veneer that makes them immune to the problems and issues we face.

After more than a decade of being a pastor, I have to admit, I love it more today than I did when we started in 2002! I love that I get to spend thirty-eight weekends a year speaking on life issues from the stage of Next Level Church. Like many churches our size, we have cameras that magnify the image of the person up front onto screens around the room and across our facility. I love getting to talk with people in the foyer after our weekend services. However, every once in a while someone approaches me with "that look."

You can always see them coming. They look at you, and then they slowly begin to walk toward you. When they get about three feet away, they say something like, "It's you! You're the guy up there!" And then they point toward the auditorium. The next comment out of their mouths is the one that always makes me laugh. I've heard people say all sorts of things: "You're a lot taller than I thought you'd be." "You look a lot younger in person." And my favorite, "You're a lot funnier up there!" Thanks. It's as if people think that I'm not like them; that I'm not a real person like they are.

Anyway, the point is, we all have this idea of what someone we admire looks like up close. And even though we know they are just regular people like we are, somehow we convince ourselves that they're different from us. That they have acquired some magical power allowing them to never struggle or deal with the issues that seem to hold us back.

MOSES, AN UNDERDOG LIKE US

In the Bible, Moses had that mystique about him. When you think about the man whom God used to deliver his people from slavery in Egypt, you think of him in celebrity tones, right? I mean, there have been movies made about him, he's been the star of animated shows, and pictures have been painted depicting his heroic actions. Heck, there's even a bobblehead of him.

It is easy to think of Moses with a plastic veneer. But as we are about to see, the man God chose to deliver his people from slavery in Egypt was anything but plastic. He *didn't* have it all figured out. He was human just like us with all his screwups, hang-ups, and mess-ups to show for it. Yet God chose to use this underdog to change the destiny of millions of people and chart the course of a nation for centuries to come.

BACKGROUND INFO

Moses had an interesting beginning to his life. He was born to a Hebrew slave woman in Egypt at the time when Pharaoh was having a panic attack. Pharaoh was worried the Hebrews were multiplying too quickly, and if he didn't begin to control the slave population, eventually they would outnumber the Egyptians, thus allowing them to take over the country by brute force.

At the time of Moses' birth, Pharaoh ordered all male babies under the age of two to be killed immediately. So Moses' mother, in a moment of sheer desperation, put baby Moses in a basket and sent him down the Nile River with the faint hope that someone would find him and be merciful to him.

As divine fate would have it, the daughter of Pharaoh found the basket, took Moses in, and then—in a way only God could orchestrate—she hired Moses' mother to become his nurse to help raise him in the palace.

What a powerful reminder of how God is at work in our lives in far more intricate ways than we could ever imagine! Just as God was perfectly orchestrating the path of Moses' life, so he is perfectly at work in the circumstances of your life. Nothing is coincidence. Absolutely nothing.

Moses was raised as a step-grandson of the most powerful man in the world. His childhood was shaped by watching and learning how Pharaoh thought, made decisions, and processed life as a high-level leader. God was truly at work in Moses' life. But then, somewhere around Moses' fortieth birthday, he began to get antsy with palace life. His heart was breaking for his people, the Hebrews, who were being forced to live as slaves in the country where he was living in privilege.

One day, while in the marketplace, Moses got into a scuffle with an Egyptian who was mistreating a Hebrew slave. One thing turned into another. Words started to fly. Fists followed.

And before the confrontation was over, Moses killed the man. He panicked and tried to hide the body, only to be confronted the next day by a fellow Hebrew man who informed Moses that he knew what Moses had done and that it wasn't going to end well.

Scared out of his mind, Moses did the only thing he knew to do. He ran! For the next forty years Moses ran. He became a fugitive. A nomad. A guy with great potential and nowhere to use it. He ended up taking a job watching sheep on a farm for a guy named Jethro, who would later become his father-in-law.

And for forty years, Moses disappeared. Out of sight. Out of commission. Too far gone. A murderer and fugitive. In Moses' mind, his rap sheet disqualified him from ever being used by God. Moses was an underdog.

TO MAKE MATTERS WORSE

As if taking a man's life wasn't bad enough, it turned out Moses didn't just have character issues he felt made him unusable; he had a personal flaw as well. Moses had an issue that would be a virtual death sentence for anyone who would be considered to influence others.

Moses stuttered.

In the 2010 movie *The King's Speech*, Colin Firth did a phenomenal job depicting the heart-stopping, gut-wrenching anxiety a leader feels when he is not able to communicate effectively with the nation he is called to lead. King George VI battled stuttering all his life.

I am confident Moses carried the weight of his stuttering

problem on his shoulders everywhere he went. Moses was insecure. He thought he was incapable. Moses was an underdog. But thankfully, what Moses saw as incapacitating, God saw differently. After all, the fate of an entire nation of people was at stake, and God wasn't about to let this underdog off the hook.

HUNTED DOWN

Moses was doing his shepherding thing as he had done for the last forty years when God found him and interrupted his peaceful little existence:

> *Now Moses was tending the flock of Jethro his father-in-law, the priest of Midian, and he led the flock to the far side of the wilderness and came to Horeb, the mountain of God. There the angel of the LORD appeared to him in flames of fire from within a bush. Moses saw that though the bush was on fire it did not burn up. So Moses thought, "I will go over and see this strange sight—why the bush does not burn up."*
>
> *When the LORD saw that he had gone over to look, God called to him from within the bush, "Moses! Moses!" And Moses said, "Here I am." (Ex. 3:1–4 NIV)*

Imagine being Moses for a moment. For forty years, you've been hiding out, minding your own business. For forty years, you've been making a life for yourself. You've got a family and responsibilities and sheep to tend. Then all of a sudden, God interrupts everything and calls to you from within a burning bush. I don't know about you, but if I were in Moses' shoes, I'd be terrified! Speaking of Moses' sandals, look what happens next:

> *"Do not come any closer,"* God said. *"Take off your sandals, for the place where you are standing is holy ground."* Then he said, *"I am the God of your father, the God of Abraham, the God of Isaac and the God of Jacob."* At this, Moses hid his face, because he was afraid to look at God.
>
> The L*ORD* said, *"I have indeed seen the misery of my people in Egypt. I have heard them crying out because of their slave drivers.... So I have come down to rescue them from the hand of the Egyptians and to bring them up out of that land into a good and spacious land, a land flowing with milk and honey.... And now the cry of the Israelites has reached me, and I have seen the way the Egyptians are oppressing them."* (Ex. 3:5–9 N*IV*)

It seemed God was in a pretty good mood, and hey, it actually sounded like God had a similar burden to Moses' burden some forty years ago. Good idea, God. But God wasn't finished: "So now, go. I am sending you to Pharaoh to bring my people the Israelites out of Egypt" (Ex. 3:10 N*IV*).

Moses must have been thinking, *I'm sorry? What's that, God? I could have sworn you just said that you wanted me to go and make that happen for you. No offense, God, but* are you crazy? *Do you have any idea what I've done and who I am? I know you're sovereign and all, but seriously, God. You've clearly made a mistake here. Maybe the smoke from the fire in the bush has clouded your vision because I am not your guy!*

DOUBTING YOURSELF

Ever felt like Moses? Maybe you've felt a tug in your heart for something. A burden for a group of people. An idea that could make a difference in your workplace, your school, or your world. But maybe, like Moses, you have felt that God must have chosen the wrong person for the job.

Maybe you've even told God all the reasons why this isn't a good idea. You've let your insecurities hold you back. That's what Moses did. For the next several minutes, because of his insecurities, Moses gave God three reasons why he was not the right choice for the job. And these three insecurities are the same ones we will face as we move toward our dreams and our destiny.

THE FIRST INSECURITY: CREDIBILITY

"Moses said to God, 'Suppose I go to the Israelites and say to them, "The God of your fathers has sent me to you," and they ask me, "What is his name?" Then what shall I tell them?'" (Ex. 3:13 NIV).

Moses felt insecure because he thought he lacked credibility. It honestly made sense to him. After all, if people started asking him why they should listen to him, he wouldn't know what to tell them. Word had surely spread about the spoiled rich kid who was not raised in slavery like everybody else. And oh yeah, don't forget he was the guy who killed someone! In Moses' mind, he had a credibility problem.

But God's response addressed this issue. "God said to Moses,

'I AM WHO I AM. This is what you are to say to the Israelites: "I AM has sent me to you"'" (Ex. 3:14 NIV).

God told Moses his credibility had nothing to do with his capability; it had everything to do with God's ability. God wanted Moses to know his credibility didn't come from who he was or what kind of past he had; it came from the reality that God had chosen him to lead this group of people.

Ever questioned your credibility? Ever felt insecure because of a lack of credibility? Perhaps you've thought, *I don't have enough experience. I don't have the upbringing or expertise like someone else.* If so, then you must know that God is your credibility. He is the great I AM. He is the one who validates what he is calling you to do.

TOO YOUNG TO BE CREDIBLE

All of my ministry life I have generally been the youngest leader in the room. With the occasional exception of somebody's son who tags along, I have spent my entire leadership career being the young guy at the table. Now, don't get me wrong. Being the young guy has its definite upsides. As a young, energetic leader, I could get away with things others couldn't. I could say things or process ideas from a different point of view from everybody else in the room without looking like the odd man out or the dissenting voice.

However, I have to admit, being the stereotypical young guy often messed with my head. I began traveling nationally at twenty-three years old, and each week I had to give myself a pep talk just to believe I had something to offer the people I was speaking to, many of whom were two or three times my age.

Then when we planted our church at the ripe old ages of twenty-six and twenty-four, I remember saying to my wife on repeated occasions, "Someday we're going to be really glad we started so young." If I'm being honest, it has taken me a long time to get over this perceived credibility issue. Perhaps you can relate. Maybe you struggle with feelings of inferiority in some area of your life. If so, know you're not alone. So did Moses. So have I.

THE SECOND INSECURITY: LACK OF EVIDENCE

As Exodus 3 ends and Exodus 4 begins, we discover Moses' second excuse: "Moses answered, 'What if they do not believe me or listen to me and say, "The LORD did not appear to you"?'" (Ex. 4:1 NIV).

Moses' second excuse that led to his insecurity was a perceived lack of evidence or proof. Moses probably thought, *Okay, sure, I can tell them the great I AM sent me. I get that, God, but what proof do I have? Isn't it going to be my word against their word?* Moses was worried he wouldn't be able to prove his leadership was God's idea.

Perhaps you've wrestled with a lack of proof in your desire to be used by God in a great way. Perhaps you've thought, *My track record is unproven. My life experience doesn't line up with what I'm feeling in my heart to do.* If so, know this: there's still hope. When we lack evidence in the natural, we can still walk confidently in the spiritual. That's called faith.

Hebrews 11:1 tells us that "faith is the substance of things hoped for, the evidence of things not seen"(KJV). In other words, we have the ability to step out, chase after our dreams, and be used mightily by God even when there's not a lot of evidence in the natural.

Seeing Moses' desire for evidence, God gave him a powerful tool to prove to everyone that God was indeed with him.

> *Then the LORD said to him, "What is that in your hand?" "A staff," he replied. The LORD said, "Throw it on the ground."*
>
> *Moses threw it on the ground and it became a snake, and he ran from it. Then the LORD said to him, "Reach out your hand and take it by the tail." So Moses reached out and took hold of the snake and it turned back into a staff in his hand. "This," said the LORD, "is so that they may believe that the LORD . . . has appeared to you." (Ex. 4:2–5 NIV)*

God gave Moses the evidence he was looking for right in the palm of his hand. God positioned Moses to be able to prove God was with him anywhere, anytime. And God is capable of doing the same for each of us. Inside us or near us is the story, experience, or proof we need to verify the calling we are feeling in our hearts. A thought, a confirming conversation, a relationship, a validation from somewhere that will act as our proof.

Now, don't panic if that proof doesn't come straight to your mind. Before God sends us out, he always brings confirmation to give us the confidence we need to begin living our big dreams for him.

PERSONAL CONFIRMATION

I remember when we were contemplating moving to southwest Florida to plant Next Level Church, we asked God for three very clear, very unique, only-God-could-do confirmations. Amazingly, within a matter of a few weeks, both Sarah and I felt that we had those confirmations.

One was a personal confirmation. One came through the organizational leaders we were working for at the time. And one was a very spiritual confirmation that gave us the confidence to step out and move 1,300 miles away from the only home we had ever known to follow this big dream God had given us to start a church.

I can't tell you in what form confirmation will come for you. There is no such thing as cookie-cutter confirmation. For Moses, it was a rod that turned into a snake. To my knowledge, God never used that confirmation again. Every person will experience different proofs that have the power to give him or her the confidence needed to step out and live the dream of God. And you are no exception.

THE THIRD INSECURITY: A PERSONAL FLAW

Moses threw one more excuse God's way. This time it was personal. "Moses said to the Lord, 'Pardon your servant, Lord. I have never been eloquent, neither in the past nor since you have spoken to your servant. I am slow of speech and tongue'" (Ex. 4:10 niv).

Moses' final pushback had to do with his stuttering problem.

Obviously, he was self-conscious about it. He was worried his inability to speak clearly to the people God was calling him to lead would be detrimental to seeing this vision from God come to pass. But God had a ready reply. "The LORD said to him, 'Who gave human beings mouths? Who makes them deaf or mute? Who gives them sight or makes them blind? Is it not I, the LORD? Now go; I will help you speak and will teach you what to say'" (Ex. 4:11–12 NIV).

God gently reminded Moses that he had nothing to fear. After all, it was God who gave Moses his tongue. In other words, God was saying to Moses, "It's not like I don't know you have a speech problem. Don't worry about it. I've got you covered." Yet Moses was unconvinced. "Moses said, 'Pardon your servant, Lord. Please send someone else'" (Ex. 4:13 NIV).

Even after the God of the universe said he had his back, Moses still wanted out! He couldn't get past his insecurity about his speech. He was willing to miss out on his destiny because of his insecurity about a personal flaw.

Well, as you might imagine, this did not sit well with God. God got angry with Moses because he was putting his personal insecurity in front of God's destiny for his life. Moses was allowing his imperfections to affect an entire nation of people, and that was not okay with God. But God didn't just leave angry. He offered a solution for Moses: "Then the LORD's anger burned against Moses and he said, 'What about your brother, Aaron the Levite? I know he can speak well. He is already on his way to meet you. . . . I will help both of you speak and will teach you what to do'"(Ex. 4:14–15 NIV).

God promised to bring others around him who could make

up for his weaknesses. God brought Aaron, Moses' brother, to be his mouthpiece.

NOW TO US

Maybe you've felt that your imperfections make you an unusable option for God. I hope you can see in the life of Moses that nothing could be further from the truth. God will be faithful to bring the people you need to accomplish the vision he has placed in your heart.

When I think about all God has accomplished since our humble beginnings in 2002, I can't help seeing faces. Yes, faces of those whom God has used Next Level Church to touch; but even more, I see the faces of the people on our team whom God has used to affect so many lives. The faces have changed quite a bit through the years, but the difference they made never leaves. I am grateful for every team member who willingly served and continues to serve the vision God placed in my heart twenty years ago.

Today, my team makes me so much better than I ever could be alone. They strengthen the areas where I'm weak and offer encouragement like crazy. I am grateful to get to do life with such dedicated, committed, loyal, fun-loving, joyful people as the staff of Next Level Church.

If God brought Aaron to Moses, and God provided the team I have to help me, he can bring you the ones you need to get the job done. Your job is to say yes! God's job is to bring you the people you need to fulfill your destiny.

It's easy to think, like Moses, that we don't have what it takes to be used by God in a great way to change our world. Maybe you don't have a stuttering problem, but you have often discredited yourself because of another personal imperfection or flaw. If so, I want you to hear this next statement:

GOD *KNEW* YOU WHEN HE *MADE* YOU, AND
HE'S NOT *LIMITED* BY YOU NOW OR EVER!

Satan would love for you to believe that because you can't speak well, because you have a disease, or because you are dyslexic or have some other imperfection, you can't be used by God. Satan would love for you to give up on your potential and throw in the towel on your dreams because you've been through a divorce or had an abortion in your past. Satan would love for you to believe that because you are wounded from an abusive relationship, you can't be the one God uses in the future.

Hear me on this: God got angry at Moses for putting his insecurities above God's ability to use him in spite of those imperfections. Moses was an underdog God chose to use to deliver his people from slavery and bondage! In the same way God wants to use your life in spite of anything you might think disqualifies you.

YOUR IMPERFECTIONS DON'T KEEP YOU
FROM YOUR DESTINY; THEY ACTUALLY
POSITION YOU PERFECTLY FOR IT!

When God uses you in spite of you, he gets all the credit. That's why God loves using underdogs! God has called you, the underdog, to be his man or woman to make an impact in your world. Stop making excuses. Stop thinking you don't have the credibility, the proof, or the ability to be who God wants you to be and to do what God wants you to do.

God is the great I AM who will go with you, and he will bring people around you to make you stronger than you ever thought you could be. God doesn't use plastic people; he uses real people. Underdogs, like Moses and like you and me, to accomplish his purposes on the earth. It is your inability, not your perfection, that makes you an underdog worth using in God's eyes.

CHAPTER 9 QR CODE (image)
**THEUNDERDOGSBOOK.COM/CH9
SCAN HERE FOR BONUS CONTENT ABOUT
"OVERCOMING THE INSECURITIES IN YOUR LIFE."**

CONCLUSION

EXCUSES ARE EVERYWHERE

Go and Change the World Anyway

{ Since we are surrounded by such a great cloud of
witnesses, let us throw off everything that hinders
and the sin that so easily entangles. And let us run
with perseverance the race marked out for us. }

HEBREWS 12:1 NIV

EVERYBODY LOVES AN UNDERDOG STORY. WHEN I TURN
on the TV and see the predictable team that is projected to win,
something inside me rises up and roots for the underdog. I think
the same thing happens with God. When he looks down on his
most prized possession in all of creation, his people, his eyes
search for the underdogs.

And when he finds some, ones like you and me, he zooms
in and begins cheering for us really hard. I believe on many days

God is shouting at the top of his lungs for us to win! I can see God cheering us on, rooting for us to overcome the excuses that try to keep us ordinary.

God didn't create you for an ordinary life. Anything but. God didn't create you so you could *not* change the world. He created you for a purpose and a destiny. But the excuses of life will try to build a wall around you. They will do everything they can to keep you inside a safe, predictable, and average life.

Don't let them stop you! Hebrews 12:1 encourages you to throw off everything that hinders and tries to entangle you. The odds may be stacked against you. People may doubt you. Voices inside you may say you're not the one. And the Enemy will be aiming at you. So as we conclude this book, I have one more piece of advice:

Excuses are everywhere. Go and
change the world anyway!

We need you. Your family needs you. Your destiny needs you. God needs you to throw off every excuse that hinders you from being the best you he made you to be.

Hebrews 12 tells us to "[fix] our eyes on Jesus, the pioneer and perfecter of faith . . . him who endured such opposition . . . so that you will not grow weary and lose heart" (vv. 2–3 NIV).

Jesus willingly endured the opposition that comes straight from the enemy of our souls, so we could live victorious lives! Jesus took on every excuse that could possibly hold us back so you and I would be encouraged, not grow weary, and not lose heart. No matter what excuse you're facing, Jesus already defeated it. When the road gets tough, and the path becomes unclear, fix your eyes on Jesus. He endured everything so we would not grow weary and lose heart. If Jesus can conquer death, we can conquer the excuses that try to hold us back.

As you conclude this book, my prayer for you is that your perspective will be forever changed. May you never believe the same about yourself again. May you see yourself in light of who God says you are and not in light of the excuses in front of you. After all, excuses are everywhere; now, go and change the world anyway.

"MY OPPONENT IS TOO GREAT"

The Ultimate Underdog

(JESUS)

TECHNICALLY, I KNOW I JUST ENDED THE BOOK, SENT YOU out with a bang, and inspired you like crazy to go live your victorious underdog life, but there's one more thing I have to share with you. It's important to me that you hear it if you really want it. So rather than just throw it into the meat of the book, I decided to add it as a "Bonus Section" for people who are interested.

So, if you feel that you've gotten what you've paid for, by all means stop reading. But if you want to hear one more angle on the whole underdog concept, the next eight minutes have the power to change your life forever.

UNDEFEATED ENEMY

Not only was Jesus the underdog with unseen potential; he was also an underdog who took on an impossible opponent. Until Jesus, the enemy of our souls, called sin, was undefeated. Sin had taken on millions of opponents and never lost. Until Jesus, sin had won every fight it ever entered, bringing down even the greatest heroes. People we've studied in this book. People like Moses, David, Gideon, and Esther. All were underdogs used by God in magnificent, world-changing ways, but ultimately, they couldn't stand before the toughest of enemies, sin.

According to the Bible, the consequence for one who takes on sin and loses is death. Each and every underdog we've explored in this book had trouble with the enemy called sin. Until Jesus. But even Jesus was an underdog in the face of such a huge foe. After all, Jesus was 100 percent God, but he was also 100 percent man. Which meant he had to fight sin on its home turf.

Sin had the home field advantage. Ever since a serpent showed up in a garden and tempted a nice young couple to eat the fruit from a tree in the middle of that garden instead of hanging out with God himself after the dishes were done, sin has had the upper hand.

Because of sin's influence on all of humanity, God knew it would require Jesus coming down, playing on sin's home turf, and defeating sin, death, hell, and the grave once and for all. And that's exactly what he did! Jesus stepped out of heaven as the underdog and lived a perfect, sinless life so you and I, average underdogs, could know what it is to have victory over the ultimate enemy of our souls: sin.

As we conclude this book, I want to give you an opportunity to respond to the ultimate underdog who took on the ultimate foe and won. If you've never said yes to a relationship with Jesus Christ, you can right now. Before you close the final pages of this book, you can know the one who defeated sin not only for his sake but also for the sake of every one of us, that we might be known by him and be called sons and daughters of God.

When we respond to a relationship with Jesus Christ, the Bible says we become sons and daughters of God: "What great love the Father has lavished on us, that we should be called children of God! And that is what we are!" (1 John 3:1 NIV).

When we acknowledge we are sinners, have missed the mark, and made mistakes, and then believe what Jesus did for us on the cross was payment for our sin, the Bible says we become new creations: "If anyone is in Christ, the new creation has come: The old has gone, the new is here!" (2 Cor. 5:17 NIV).

Because Jesus, the underdog, defeated sin when he rose from the dead, we can know what it is to have eternal life. It is as simple as praying a prayer from your heart right now. When you take one step in God's direction, he takes ninety-nine in your direction. Let me encourage you to open your heart right now, and pray this prayer:

Dear Jesus, thank you for coming to this earth as the ultimate underdog and dying on the cross for my sin. Thank you for loving and enduring that so I could be known by the Father. I acknowledge when I'm left to myself, I go my own way, and that path never leads me where I want to go.

I ask you to forgive me of my sin. Wash me clean, and make me a new creation. Today, I begin a relationship with you. I want you to be first in my life. I yield control of my life to you and invite you to lead me, an underdog, into the great life you have for me. In Jesus' name I pray. Amen.

If you prayed that prayer and meant it from your heart, you must know God heard you and has done the work in you. You are forgiven of your past, your failures, and your screwups. According to the Bible, you have just moved from orphan status to member-of-the-family status in the family of God. Congratulations!

WHERE DO YOU GO FROM HERE?

Now that you're in relationship with God, you must begin to live out that relationship with him. Here are a couple of steps to take immediately:

1. FIND MORE UNDERDOGS.

God doesn't want us to live life alone. He created the local church so you and I could live out our underdog journey with others who are on the same journey of faith. Find a good church in your city. One where you feel that you can grow in your faith and use your gifts to serve others.

2. BEGIN READING AND APPLYING THE BIBLE TO YOUR EVERYDAY LIFE.

By far the greatest way to grow in your relationship with God is by reading and applying his Word, the Bible, to your everyday life. If you don't have a Bible, get one. You can buy one wherever books are sold or even download the free YouVersion Bible app on your smartphone. It has never been easier to access the Word of God in your life.

[God] created the local church so you and I could live out our underdog journey with others who are on the same journey of faith.

But here's what I've found. Reading alone won't necessarily affect you and bring about the life change you seek. Until you learn to apply the Word of God to your life, you'll never become all God wants you to become. The simplest and most effective way I've ever found to do that is through a method called SOAP. The acronym is easy to use and yet powerful for everyday life. It stands for Scripture, observation, application, and prayer.

Here's how it works. Regardless of how much of the Bible you read each day, the goal is to find one verse each day you feel is speaking to you and write it down in a journal or notebook. (That's the *S* for Scripture.) Then, write down what you see in the verse. (That's the *O* for observation.) Next, write down how you feel this applies to your life. (That's the *A* for application.) And finally, turn your observation and application into a dedication. In other words, write out a prayer to God of how you're going to live your life differently because of this verse today. (That's the *P* for prayer.)

It really is simple and yet powerful at the same time. Though the concept was not originally ours, we actually created an *Intro to SOAP* guide that has now helped tens of thousands of people learn how to study the Bible and apply it to their lives using this method. For more information or to order one, go to www .IntroToSOAP.com.

Let me say thank you for taking the extra eight minutes to read this bonus section of *God of the Underdogs*. I trust it has been a life-changing and worthwhile experience for you. By the way, I would love to hear how God has used this book or even this particular bonus section to impact your life. Feel free to find me on Twitter at @MatthewKeller.

Thanks for reading. Now go and live the victorious underdog life God has designed for you!

Matt Keller

ACKNOWLEDGMENTS

FIRST, FOR THE SERIOUS ONES:

To Dick Harp, who told me to "stay in the Book," so I did. This one's for you, Dick!!! I love you, man. Thanks for your support from day one! You and Sharon mean the world to us. Thanks for always telling me, "You haven't seen anything yet!"

To my mom and dad, your constant belief in me made me believe I could change the world. Thanks for doing so many things right in our childhood. If everyone could have had the parents I had, the world would be a different place today. Thanks for setting me up to achieve my dreams.

To Sarah, you're truly a gracious and beautiful woman. Thanks for "taking the entire journey with me . . ." You're my butterfly. I love who you've become and who we get to be together. Do you think they can tell we're having the time of our lives?

To my boys, Will and Drew, you guys are underdogs in your generation, and I can't wait to see what God has for you in the years ahead. I'm so proud of the men you are becoming!

To Mike Ash, can you believe it? I sure am glad we didn't give up, even when they were giving up on us! Thanks for being my Jonathan. I wouldn't want to do any of this without you.

To Blythe Daniel, my agent. Seriously, you are a hawk. I'm so thankful that God put us together. You're partnership with me and belief in this project made it happen. Thanks for being my "hawk"!

To Kyle and Jen Jackson, you two represent the best of what is great about the next generation. I believe in you more than you know. You're world-changing underdogs in the greatest way!

To Chelsie and Cheri, my assistants. Yeah, you know who runs "Matt's World." I would be a scattered mess without both of you. Thanks for keeping me organized and on time.

To my mother-in-law, Alison. You help our family in so many ways. We couldn't do what we do without you. You are truly the perfect "houseguest"!

To our tribe of pastors and leaders around the country who believe in me and follow us. We have you in mind in everything we do. Don't worry, we'll keep taking good notes.

To the staff of Next Level Church, you make it a joy to come to work every day (except Fridays!). Your won't-take-no-for-an-answer attitudes make it possible for us to do all we do! Your excitement around this book and the underdogs message has kept me going. I love the culture we're creating together.

To my Next Level Church family, I had no idea that a church family could be this healthy and exciting and fun. This really is what life in God's kingdom is all about. Thanks for taking this journey with us.

To the next generation, this book is for you. My life is dedicated to you. You are "the elect" God has called me to give my life to (2 Timothy 2:10). I really do believe you can change the world. Let me know how I can help you do that better.

———

NOW, FOR SOME BREVITY:

To Diet Coke, you were my constant companion through this project. Sorry I cheated on you occasionally with Red Bull. To Apple, yeah, you gave me the ability to write this book on my laptop, iPad, and iPhone. That's sweet. To the guys who wrote/put together (however you say that) the NIV translation of the Bible, I like it. I really do. Thanks for doing that. To the Tampa Bay Rays, I love the way you've built the team. Superb. We just need a new stadium and we're home free! Call me, I think I can help. To the snowbirds who visit southwest Florida every year, thanks for helping our economy, but could you drive a little faster? Seriously. To my homeowners association, thanks for cutting my grass, and for not fining me for parking in the street sometimes. To my hero, John Maxwell. You simply have no idea how you've impacted my life. To Seth Godin, you inspire me every day. You think about things like nobody else on the planet. I love that. To Billy Hornsby, thanks for believing in us when no one else did. To the makers of my reading glasses, gosh, where would I be without you? To the creators of the free white-noise app, you made it possible to block out distractions that would have caused this ADD boy to go crazy. To Post-it, thanks for making those giant Post-its that stick to the walls. You've changed my life forever. To the inventor of the DVR, seriously man, you changed my world too.

I'm more efficient with you than I ever was without you. To the TV executives who think the World Series games should start so late and have so many commercials, I think you've got it wrong this time, you guys. Call me. For the sake of the children.

———

AND LAST BUT NOT LEAST:

Thanks to God. You took an underdog kid and used me to impact lives. I could not have asked for a better life than the one you've given me. Thank you for my three callings: to pastor, to write, and to lead at a high level. I can't believe I get to do what I do every day. Not only am I having a blast, but I'm giving the best part of me, in the best years of my life, to the thing that's closest to your heart . . . people. I couldn't ask for more, well, maybe one thing . . . if you could think about adding a few more hours to the day, that would be awesome. Twenty-four is good and all, but some days I could really use, like, thirty. Just a thought. I mean, I'm good with whatever, though. Thanks for letting me be an underdog you're using.

I love you, Lord.

Matt

ABOUT THE AUTHOR

MATT KELLER IS THE PASTOR OF NEXT LEVEL CHURCH (www.NextLevelChurch.com), the church he planted in 2002 in Fort Myers, Florida. He is also the author of the book *The Up the Middle Church*, a book designed for leaders and churches to do ministry more effectively one yard at a time. Matt travels and speaks often and is passionate about coaching pastors nationwide. Out of that passion, he founded the Next Level Coaching Co in 2006. Matt writes frequent leadership articles on his website, www.MattKellerOnline.com, and can be followed on Twitter @MatthewKeller. Matt and his wife, Sarah, live in Fort Myers, Florida, with their two boys, Will and Drew. Matt's favorite candy continues to be Skittles.